THE NATURE OF FAITH

GERHARD EBELING

THE NATURE OF
FAITH

TRANSLATED BY
RONALD GREGOR SMITH

FORTRESS PRESS   PHILADELPHIA

First published as *Das Wesen des Christlichen Glaubens* by J. C. B. Mohr (Paul Siebeck), Tübingen, 1959.

Copyright © Gerhard Ebeling and J. C. B. Mohr (Paul Siebeck), Tübingen, 1959
Copyright © in the English translation Wm. Collins Sons & Co. Ltd., 1961

Library of Congress Catalog Card Number 62-7194
ISBN 0-8006-1914-5

First American Edition 1961 by Fortress Press
First American paperback edition 1967 by Fortress Press
Second printing 1969
Third printing 1980

8284E80   Printed in the United States of America   1-1914

Foreword

This book contains a course of lectures which I gave in the winter of 1958/59 at the University of Zürich for students of all faculties. As an Appendix I have added a lecture which I gave on the 22nd February, 1959, over the South German radio, and which was printed in the *Neue Zürcher Zeitung* (8/3/59). As regards time and contents it is of a piece with the course.

I have left untouched the character of the spoken word. I have not attempted to elaborate what I have often said too briefly, or to fill in the many gaps. A task of this kind would be unlimited and would completely alter my original intention. My intention was not to present complete dogmatics, but to give an introduction to the understanding of Christian faith. For this task formal completeness was not necessary. The attentive reader has both the right and the duty to try to fill in the outlines that are presented here.

My friend, Ernst Fuchs, has read the manuscript and by many criticisms and much encouragement has eased the path to publication. My assistant, Thomas Bonhoeffer, was untiring in his labours to improve the form. To both of these I should like to express my hearty thanks.

GERHARD EBELING

Zürich, 1st June, 1959

Contents

I

The Question about the Nature of Christian Faith

It is both a necessary and a hazardous undertaking to put the question about the nature of Christian faith, or, as we should rather say, to face this question. This apparently trivial change in the form of the problem expresses the fact that we are dealing with a question which includes a definite kind of participation.

Every question which we deal with presupposes some kind of participation, some "interest," as we say. The Latin word *interesse* means literally to be between, to be there, to be concerned in something, to share in it. Now, there are many different kinds of questions. They can be classified not only according to the difference in the objects which are in question, but also according to the different way in which the questioner is interested in the question, the way he shares in it, the way in which he is there. The interest of the questioning can be sheer curiosity. It can also be a genuine desire for knowledge. In the first case, we are asking about something which, strictly speaking, does not concern us, even though in our curiosity we are burningly interested in it. In the second case we are asking about something that concerns us only in a definite connection, for example, when we study an insect from the standpoint of its behaviour and try to explain the phenomena which we observe. It is true that this is usually called a questioning without participation. But even pure observation of this kind is strictly a very lively form of participation, even though it is governed by a specific interest.

But there are questions of yet another kind, namely, those which concern me, not merely in this or that way but in my very being; for example, if I ask about the spiritual situation of the present, or what love really means, or what death is. Even if I myself am not explicitly mentioned when such questions are asked, nevertheless they can only be discussed if I myself am in fact brought into the conversation. This is because they are questions which actually concern me, for I myself appear in them, I myself am called in question in them.

The question about the nature of Christian faith is of this latter kind. This is not an arbitrary assertion, it is not a preacher's trick to lay claim to you, but it is simply the appropriate structure of the question. It would be inappropriate, even nonsensical, to put the question about the nature of Christian faith from curiosity or as a mere question of knowledge. It would likewise be meaningless to regard the question, say, of death merely as one which concerned my curiosity or my thirst for knowledge, and not as one which concerned me in the sense that I myself must die. Of course, I am not suggesting that this particular question has an absolutely special place. The circle of questions which concern man in his very being as man, and in which therefore the questioner himself is included, is a very large one. For the present we simply say that there are questions which we do not rightly see if we leave ourselves out of them, if, that is to say, we refuse the commitment which is part of the nature of these questions, if we are to be concerned with them in the way that is appropriate to them.

But what does it mean, that I myself appear in these questions and that therefore a definite commitment is demanded of me, if I am to go into them properly? It means that I am part of the sphere of what is being asked. The answer to questions of this

kind necessarily contains something about myself. Further, since I am both the one who asks and part of what is being asked about, I am at the same time the one who is asked, challenged for an answer, and who has to be answerable for the answer that is to be given. We have to deal here with a kind of question which cannot be answered without the inclusion of a personal standpoint, in the answering of which I therefore make myself known to a certain extent. For the answering of the question my own commitment is therefore required. I must identify myself with the answer so that it is I myself who am answerable for it, I allow myself to be made responsible.

That is why such questions cannot be answered once for all and thereby settled. The question, let us say, about the sum of the angles in a triangle is settled once for all, and strictly speaking is no longer a question. But this question which is to concern us is one of those which continually has to be put, the answering of which is never settled once for all. Let me repeat that I am not describing a state of affairs which only holds in the question about the nature of Christian faith. Every genuine philosophical question, indeed every question which concerns human life, and therefore in the broadest sense history, is of this nature—that is, every question which cannot be settled by mere statements and explanations, but which has understanding as its goal. Understanding is always accomplished in a kind of dialogue and must therefore be won ever anew, but must also be hazarded ever anew. That is why philosophy must always begin anew and history must always be written anew. For the same reason theology must always be carried on anew and must—that is why it is there—be preached ever anew.

It looks as though in our first reflections upon the question of the nature of Christian faith, things and standpoints had suddenly merged with one another which we normally keep widely separated, as having nothing to do with one another, or as being hostile to one another. It may not be surprising that when speaking of Christian faith we should say that some kind of participation is necessary, some kind of confession or commitment. But it may be surprising that I should identify the matter with our attitude towards philosophical and historical questions in general. The personal element in this matter can be readily acknowledged. But it is perhaps somewhat disturbing that I should immediately connect this with the historicity of our human life, which is so much a matter of subjectivity and relativity. Is it not possible to answer the question about the nature of Christian faith plainly and clearly, in unambiguous objectivity, and with absolute correctness, valid once for all? Whereas it looks (on my view) as though every individual were being made responsible for the answer and as if one saw no end to the concern about this question.

I am conscious of the danger that what I have so far said cannot yet be properly assimilated, or grasped in its full significance, with the consequence that nothing more than a certain mood is established—namely, a feeling of discomfort, of strangeness, like our sensations during a mild earthquake. " What has actually happened? " we ask ourselves, " nothing seems to have changed," and yet we have the sensation that there has been some kind of shaking, not one of the normal superficial shakings, but a shaking of the very foundations. This is precisely what I mean: this uncanny sensation that the very foundations could move is part of the beginning of our question about the nature of Christian faith.

That was the purpose of the remark with which I began, that it is an undertaking which is both necessary and hazardous, to put the question about the nature of Christian faith. It is necessary because there can be no faith without understanding. It is hazardous because we might become aware how deep our misunderstanding and our lack of understanding go, whether we affirm the Christian faith or reject it. For this is the risk which one takes in raising this question. It is possible that on a closer examination things are different from what one had hitherto imagined. Ideas that we had thought to be self-evident could break up. Our attitude to the Christian faith and thereby our own existence could begin to move in a way that we did not like at all. A transformation in our thinking and understanding could be demanded which we would not know how to endure. Moreover, as I say, this is true for both groups, for the adherents as well as for the opponents of the Christian faith—not to forget the third group, the well-intentioned neutrals. Everyone has his idea of what Christian faith is. This is the basis of his attitude. This idea must not be touched if one's attitude is neither to falter nor be revised. It is not only the adherents of the Christian faith who think they know all about it and therefore try to immunise themselves as far as possible from any further questioning. It is also true of the decided opponents of Christian faith that their position depends on a specific understanding of Christian faith. To question this understanding seems to them to be a tiresome suggestion, which is of course meaningless from the start. Even the great numbers of distant well-wishers of the Christian faith who readily admit that they understand little about it are indifferent or resigned or agnostic because they have reached a position in which they have basically settled the problem, or at any rate expect precious little from any more detailed questioning.

Genuine, open, honest and expectant questioning about the nature of Christian faith is something rare, and makes an extraordinarily hard demand of anyone who is familiar with Christianity. I cannot guarantee that in this course I shall succeed in holding fast to the question as I ought to, or that I can carry others along with me in this kind of openness of questioning. No doubt we will experience the power there is in stubborn clinging to alleged self-evident truths, and the strength of resistance to any demand really to expose ourselves to this question. Perhaps the unpredictable will also happen, and here and there something will be set in motion and at least there will be an inkling of what awaits us, rather, approaches us, of understanding in relation to the Christian faith. It seems to me that our time provides every reason for reaching a new and real understanding of what Christian faith is about; for what I said about the risk in our question underlines its necessity. He who is seriously concerned about the Christian faith should realise the urgency of this question about understanding. I should like to illustrate this point by describing some experiences that are open to everyone.

First, to understand what Christian faith is about, certain knowledge is essential. If, by means of certain test questions, we were able to construct a picture of what the average man of to-day knows of Christianity and what kind of ideas he has of its nature, then I think that by and large we would find a shocking ignorance. When I say the man of to-day, I am thinking of him in his many different guises, as engineer and doctor, as merchant and artist, as farmer and civil servant, as industrial worker and professor, as teacher and housewife, as churchgoer and unchurched. People like to talk to-day in exalted tones of the Christian West and in face of danger from the East they like to speak of Christianity partly as that which must unconditionally be defended and partly as that which ought to mobilise the powers of resistance. I do not want at the moment to consider the correctness of such views. But it is, at any rate, incongruous that what is meant by Christianity is only very vaguely understood. As a matter of general education we ought to be better informed. We in the West have every reason to ask whether we do not treat the Christian faith too cavalierly, making use of it in a rhetorical and ideological fashion, without really knowing what it is about.

Secondly, the guilt for this state of affairs is certainly to be in large measure ascribed to what the church itself says. We need only think of the religious instruction and the confirmation classes which go on year after year, generation after generation. Of course there are shining exceptions. But for the most part this instruction does not even fulfil the basic demand for reliable information, and one must unhappily ask whether it does not do more harm than good. Is the situation any better when we consider the sermons? Again it is undeniable that on occasion something decisive happens here. And it must never be forgotten that what really happens cannot be controlled or measured statistically. Nevertheless, we need only consider our own experiences quite coolly in order to conclude that we have to bring a certain measure of good will to the average sermon, if we are not to be bored or furious, sarcastic or melancholy in our reactions. What an expenditure of effort is put into the preaching of the Christian faith up and down the land! But—again with exceptions—is it not the institutionally assured platitudes which are preached? It would clearly be wrong to reproach individual ministers and teachers of religion for this state of affairs. Of course there are failures in this as in all professions. But here, perhaps more than in other professions, there is also sacrificial suffering. One usually describes as martyrs only those who have suffered death in public persecutions of Christians. But there is also a moving story of hidden martyrdom in manses and vicarages and in the teaching of religion, as a consequence of the indolence of Christians in our time.

But neither individual devotion nor individual failure is the root of this whole situation. From a purely objective standpoint, the peculiar difficulty in the task of Christian preaching to-day surely lies in the fact that it sounds like a foreign language. Individual words and sentences can of course be understood. Indeed, they are perhaps so familiar that they do not arouse much thought, or at any rate they do not provoke astonishment or reflection. This state of affairs may even be prized and regarded as a criterion of orthodoxy. But the import of this, in relation to the reality which surrounds and concerns us, remains uncomprehended. It would be quite wrong to say that we understand the Christian faith in and for itself, and that we lack only the relation which must be established with present reality. Rather, the criterion for understanding what Christian faith is about is to be found in the actual affecting of our real situation, not just in the subsequent consideration of it. For Christian faith is concerned precisely with this real life of ours. But we are accustomed to have Christian preaching tell of another reality than our own, and at best to look for connections between the two as an afterthought.

Christians have become accustomed to existence in two spheres, the sphere of the church and the sphere of the world. We have become accustomed to the co-existence of two languages, Christian language with the venerable patina of two thousand years, and the language of real life round about us. Certainly, it may happen that the spark of understanding leaps across the gap. But there are no comprehensive rules for translating from the one language to the other. We need not emphasise that the problem lies too deep to be tackled by cheap borrowing of transient modern jargon for the preacher's stock of words. It is not a matter of understanding single words, but of understanding the word itself, not a matter of new means of speech, but of a new coming to speech.

It is true that this is a problem which is always present to Christian communication. But to-day it is acute to an unprecedented degree. For about three hundred years our world has been involved in a revolution of unheard-of extent. What we are going through to-day is only a phase of a revolution which goes much farther back, though undoubtedly a specially stirring phase, which can make even the sleepiest of us aware of what has been going on long before our own time. For even if we are catching up only very slowly in our consciousness, whether we want to be or not we are all people of this changed world, living in it, marked by it, and responsible for it. The language of our Christian preaching, on the other hand, and the way in which Christian faith is understood and expressed, spring from the period preceding that great revolution. This is not an argument against Christian faith; but it presents a task of interpretation the magnitude of which is certainly glimpsed, but of which only the first beginnings have been tackled. We must be clear that there can be no understanding of the Christian faith unless this task is undertaken.

Thirdly and lastly, as a direct consequence of what I have just said, the remarkable tension of our life in two spheres, which now appears to be also a life in two times (in the present, and in a specific phase of the church's past), creates quite irregular appearances and dangerous distortions. If we study the atheist propaganda of Eastern Europe we are horrified at the low level and the crudeness of the arguments, which completely miss the point of Christian faith. But the dreadful thing is that what is attacked with such poisonous mockery is something that Christian ignorance has for long enough held, and in places still does hold, to be the nature of Christian faith, and perhaps under the influence of these attacks now to be defended as essential. All the old questions about the Bible and science, which should have been long settled, have suddenly acquired a melancholy virulence. For example, the question whether man is descended from the apes has recently become a subject of controversy among Christians in the Eastern Zone of Germany. This is only an illustration of the general situation.

The understanding of what Christian faith is has been made difficult, and even impossible, by problems which should have been settled long ago, since they are not the genuine problems at all. In general, what happens is the same as the development of an individual into an adult. If in matters of faith he does not grow out of his childhood ideas, these ideas become childish. These checks in Christian growth are dangerous, because they lead to the separation of faith from understanding, and indeed to the confusion of lack of understanding, and renunciation of understanding, with faith. But a faith which shirks the question of understanding is not real faith. This is evident in the yoking of faith with fear, *angst*. A fearfulness, which contradicts faith, is an ominous modern symptom of Christianity.

These preliminary remarks are simply intended to raise questions. We must take courage for critical thought. That is why I speak of the *nature* of Christian faith. By this historically heavily burdened idea of nature we mean, in the first instance, just what Christian faith really means, what makes it Christian faith. We must try to experience and understand this in critical distinction from everything that is unessential and much that is wrong, which has got confused with Christian faith. So we have to attempt a critique which the Christian faith itself urges upon us—just as understanding is disclosed in faith itself.

I propose to treat in turn the great themes of Christian faith: Jesus, Faith in Christ, God, the Word of God, The Holy Spirit, Man, Justification, Love, the Church, the World, Temptation and Hope. But first, in order to get our bearings, I must speak of Church History and Scripture.

II

The History of Faith

My choice of themes looks as though it had been made with the intention of ensuring the discussion of the chief *objects* of the Christian faith. If this were so, the plan would already indicate an answer to the question of the nature of Christian faith. Faith would then be, if I may say so, an empty sack whose nature it is to serve as a container for specific objects. If it contains the prescribed Christian objects of faith, then it is Christian faith. If it contains them complete and undamaged, then it is orthodox Christian faith. But if only a few meagre objects are contained in it, and moreover not in quite correct form, then the faith is in a bad way. For the essential thing about faith is its content. He who is in earnest about faith is intent on filling the sack full, and taking over everything that is the necessary content of faith, even if he collapses under the burden. Someone who is less conscientious has a somewhat easier life, but he has the uneasy feeling that so far as Christian faith is concerned he has not done his full stint.

In some such way as this Christian faith is usually understood. The question about its nature may then be more precisely formulated: What all must one believe?

This view is a terrible misunderstanding, which has caused immeasurable havoc. It has eaten so deep into our understanding that it is scarcely possible to oppose it without being grossly misunderstood. For if we deny that faith is an achievement, we merely seem to be proposing a loose conception of faith. And if we reject the idea that faith is the intellectual appropriation of arbitrary assertions, and even put a question-mark against the phrase "*object* of faith," then we come under the suspicion of dissolving faith in mood and feeling. But in truth the objection to the common misunderstanding is intended to assert the genuine reliance of faith on preaching and doctrine. And it is intended to make clear how everything depends in strict exclusiveness upon faith, so that one can say that in faith a life-and-death decision is taken.

With this preamble I merely wish to indicate that the formulation of our theme as a whole, its meaning and its sub-divisions, express a view which is not simply self-evident, and which I must summarily present in the following three propositions.

First, the decisive thing in Christianity is faith. In line with the famous lectures by Adolf von Harnack at the turn of the century, I could indeed have formulated the theme as "The Essence of Christianity." But I thought I might try to be more precise. If we ask about the essence of Christianity, then we must ask about the essence of Christian faith. However confusing the manifold historical forms in which Christianity makes its appearance in the different centuries and different parts of the earth, the different nations and civilisations, the different confessions and personalities, however repulsive the contentions about faith, and however attractive only so-called practical Christianity may seem, nevertheless there cannot be the least doubt that Christianity itself has at all times and in all places regarded faith as constituting its essence. He who becomes a Christian has always been asked, do you believe? It is therefore no arbitrary constriction to point the question as we do at Christian faith.

Second, Christian faith is not a special faith, but simply faith. Admittedly, as a preliminary thesis this is much less illuminating. But the history of the word "faith" indicates that we are not dealing with a religious word of universal occurrence, but that the concept of faith comes from the Old Testament, and obtained in Christianity its central and decisive significance. And Christian faith itself always wished to be basically understood as containing the true fulfilment of the meaning of faith. Hence the word "faith" can be widely used in an absolute sense, without any explanatory addition. Any more detailed additions serve simply to clarify the origin, basis, reality and life of this faith. Therefore when we simply speak in what follows of "the faith," then we mean Christian faith, but with the implication that it is true faith, simply faith, just as Christian love is not a special kind of love, but true love, simply love.

Finally, if in all that follows we are not dealing with a more or less random collection of individual objects and propositions which have simply to be believed and gathered together in faith as though it were a container, if, rather, everything serves to illuminate the nature of faith itself, then all the time we are concerned with one single thing. And this single thing must be allowed to appear in all that is said, through a strict regard for the inner connection. That is why I have used the word "faith" in the title of each lecture, though in different connections. For faith is movement and happening, it is life, fulfilled life. The title "the history of faith" could also serve for the whole account; for in dealing with faith it deals with the history of faith. Perhaps this usage, "history of faith," is surprising, so let me elucidate it now.

The predominant view is that history and faith have, strictly speaking, nothing to do with one another, and if they do have a connection then it is finally disclosed as a contradiction between faith and history. Faith is supposed to be a turning away from the restlessness and busyness of the world and a turning towards the stillness and peace of the divine, a turning from this world to the world beyond, from the temporal to the eternal, from the transient and unreliable to the permanent and reliable, from the historical to the supra-historical. For it is history which seems to be the aggregate of the vicissitudes of the human race in temporality and finitude, and therefore to be that which passes away, whereas faith in contrast to this seems to be the achievement of stability in that which does not pass away.

But this opposition leads to a mortal conflict. History, as far as its course may be seen, is clearly disclosed as the greater power, and as simply superior. If the struggle for power between history and faith is measured by the practical results, by what is realised of faith, what assertions of faith are historically confirmed, what hopes of faith are fulfilled, then history appears all along the line as the refutation of faith. This has with some justification been shown to happen at the very beginning of Christianity. Jesus, and the early Christians, thought that the end of history and the coming of the kingdom of God were immediately imminent; they were clearly deceived. The history of the church, it is said, arose on the basis of this disillusion. Or, as has been also said, Jesus proclaimed the kingdom of God—but it was the church which came! We shall not discuss this thesis, but use it simply as an illustration, which we must take quite seriously, of how faith appears in history. The question which has always been lying in wait—whether a sober experience of reality and a serious understanding of history in its historicity do not end in the refutation of faith, not just in this or that point, such as the expectation of the imminent end of the world, but in respect of the nature of faith—in modern times this question has leapt out upon men like a beast of prey, it has come upon them like fate or (whatever view one takes of it) has brought about the great disenchantment, disillusionment and radical secularisation, whose effects no one can escape. For now the illusion of a Christian world is over, and likewise the ersatz kingdom of God on earth which the social gospellers dreamed of. We have to decide, for history or for faith.

If we hold to history, and stand on its side, then it seems difficult, if not impossible, simultaneously to hold fast to faith. No need to oppose faith with wild fanaticism; one may also mourn its gradual disappearance. For this is the most moving thing about the modern revolt of history against faith, that faith itself becomes something that is, as is commonly said, "merely historical," that faith and its utterances and conceptions are understood and indeed thoroughly appreciated in a historical way, but that it is thereby delivered up to the transience of history. And how can this be contradicted? The Bible, for example, is from a historical point of view very remote from us. Theology least of all is in a position to deny this. What an effort of historical learning is required for the understanding of this book! And even in its contemporary utterances the church has so many historical trappings that anyone who is unfamiliar with it regards an encounter with it as an encounter with past centuries. Even the various hymn books have to be printed with some explanatory notes, because the language of the hymns is not that of our time but of a previous century. The church has often been accused of being a museum. It is indeed not a sign of education, to use the words "historical museum" as a kind of abuse. But even if we take account of what is honourable and edifying in the historical, it is certainly fatal for the church to be respected merely as a museum. On the other hand, a church which is ashamed of the historical, and which tries to be modern, is all the more at the mercy of time's vicissitudes. But if faith is nothing but a historical expression, then may it not be something entirely transitory, so that—as is said plainly enough—the age of faith has passed for ever?

But if, nevertheless, we still hold fast to faith, then there seems to be no other choice than to turn away from history. It is true that in earthly and worldly matters we are inextricably involved in history. But so far as possible we remain disinterested, and take refuge on an island of faith, where at any rate subjectively we keep the problem of history at bay. Not a few people see in this attitude a return to the truly Christian standpoint, while they regard entering into the world and history as the great sin of Christianity. On this view faith still clings to at least one thread of history, which is considered to be very different from the other threads of which the web of history consists, namely, the so-called salvation-history contained in the Bible, which is indispensable to Christian faith—unless one turns decisively away from this as well and separates faith completely (if one may still call it "faith") from history, and understands it idealistically or mystically as the grasping of the eternal in immediacy. For as Lessing has so emphatically said, accidental truths of history can never be a proof of necessary truths of reason.

But in spite of all this there does take place to-day the public preaching of faith, and connected with it, confession of faith. And in virtue of this the community of faith continues and is formed ever anew. Certainly it is very questionable; yet in such a way that we can take this idea of "questionable" quite literally: it is worth the trouble to question this modern existence of Christian faith about its basis. In view of the witness of faith that can be heard in our time, in view of the Christian martyrdom that is suffered, far beyond the little that we know of, hidden away, yet not on a quiet island, and in view of the manifold holding fast of faith—in view of all this, and in spite of all the problems attached to it, it would be shamelessly superficial to ignore it as a mere relic of the past, a mere inconsistent passing by of life in the present and a thoughtless ignoring of the significance of history.

I have deliberately called attention to what actually is happening. Of course it is ambiguous, as all events are. But it is noteworthy that faith to-day, as always, appears as an event. For this reason the relation between faith and history is perhaps different, even radically different, from what is commonly supposed.

We must first note something that is both simple and basic: faith comes to us out of history, and it takes us into its history. Even what we are doing here is a participation in the history of faith. For faith is not some kind of innate truth of reason, which we may come upon of ourselves and which we can recall as we please. Nor is it a purely inward happening which concerns us solely in our private existence. Rather, faith comes into being as the consequence of the witness of faith. And it depends for its nourishment on the constantly renewed witness, the Word of faith. That is to say, it comes into being, and continues in being, when it is handed on, in tradition. However manifold the effects and consequences of faith, its primal and real expression consists in its holding to the fact that it is faith. That is, it holds by the place of its origin, it confesses its origin, it declares that it is bound once for all to this its origin, in a simple once-for-all decision, in the way that only birth and death, of all that may happen in history, are simply once-for-all. That is why birth and death must help to explain what happens in baptism. For we are bound to speak of baptism, of being fitted into an unbroken chain of historical succession of believers, and of living and acting and bearing and suffering and rejoicing together in a specific concrete community, if we are to speak aright of faith. But we must postpone this discussion, as well as the question about the grounds for the assertion that faith is so dependent upon tradition, and must be so completely taken up into a specific historical context —in other words, to put it in terms of a single name, why Jesus Christ must be preached if faith is to be disclosed and its nature and activity are to be maintained.

It may sound shocking to describe the basic relation of faith and history as a dependence of faith on tradition. Perhaps we have in mind that it is Roman Catholic to put tradition alongside (and then in practice superior to) Scripture, while it is Protestant to give sole authority to Scripture. I do not intend to blur the profound difference which does exist in the understanding of Christian faith; but I want to get rid of rigid formulas. What else is Scripture but a piece of historical tradition? Moreover, Protestant insistence upon " Scripture alone " does not mean that the historical course of faith is identical with the distribution of bibles. It is the Reformation insight that faith comes from the spoken word, that is, that the message—though certainly coming from the Bible and drawing from its text and confirmed by its text—is handed on from man to man, from nation to nation by word of mouth, one might even say, personally, not anonymously, in such a way that the witness is entirely exposed and ready for the utmost surrender. He is not like a postman, who just delivers letters whose contents he does not know; nor like a herald, who ceremoniously reads out a proclamation; but he is like a responsible deputy who has been given full powers to speak. If the word of faith—which the New Testament calls the gospel—had not reached us in this way, by word of mouth, by being passed on personally, then we should know nothing about faith.

And just as we must not isolate Scripture from the later history of the proclamation of the gospel, neither can we give it an independent life in face of the event to which it bears witness. The tradition on which faith is dependent is not a law of faith, but the attestation of an event of faith. What is handed down is certainly also a demand of faith, but first it is lived faith. Scripture bears witness to Jesus as the "pioneer and perfecter of faith" (Hebrews 12.2). And Paul sees in what has happened in Jesus, namely, that faith has come in him, i.e. is disclosed for the whole world, the fulfilment of the promise to Abraham, who stands at the beginning of Israel's history as the father of faith, and awaits from all nations his promised successors in faith. That faith and history belong together cannot be made plainer than in Abraham's leaving his home to go into the unknown, following a behest which sent him on his way in expectation and hope. What else is this existence of Abraham in faith but the acceptance of truly historical existence? And from that point, if the biblical witness is right, a great arch swings to Jesus, and from Jesus to us.

And yet to speak of a history of faith still sounds somewhat objectionable to us. For as we have seen, a history of faith does not just mean the constantly recurring event of faith, but it points to a context of tradition. But history is surely not changeless. Then does the fact of a history of faith not exclude the point of tradition, namely, the maintenance of the original in unchanged purity? In that case are there not just two possibilities left, either deformation or evolution? If one thinks of church history, it is not difficult to interpret it from the standpoint of deformation. We need only construct a few phrases with faith, to throw light on the wretchedness of church history: errors of faith, contentions of faith, compulsion of faith, division of faith, war of faith, poverty of faith, atrophy of faith. It is no accident that one of the main preoccupations in modern historical writing and the awakening historical consciousness is with church history as a history of scandal, whether the scandal of divided Christendom, or the scandal of worldliness with a religious camouflage, or the scandal of a religiously justified abandonment to sheer worldliness. Yet it cannot be denied that in the history of the church there has also been apparent from time to time something of the genuine scandal of the cross and of the true freedom of the sons of God. Should then the other view of historical change, that of evolution, not be summoned to help us here? The fear which is aroused by the idea of a development of revelation beyond that of the New Testament—whether in the enthusiasm of the high-flyers or the enlightened form of modern evolutionary thought, or indeed also in certain tendencies in the Roman Catholic understanding of tradition—should not prevent us from finding a grain of truth even in this view.

Admittedly, it is only possible to entertain the thought of a higher religious development beyond Jesus Christ if you do not understand that Jesus did not come in order to found a new religion, but in order to waken faith—if you do not understand the difference between religion and faith. To understand this difference will be one of the tasks of this whole discussion of the nature of faith. Nor do we wish to discuss at present the development of individual historical manifestations of Christianity. These are of course to be found in every possible direction, in cultural forms, in sociological structures, in theology, and so on. If this were not the case, the history of the church would of course not be history at all.

But the question is whether we must speak of a historical change in faith itself. To this we reply, first, that we must certainly talk of change in respect of faith, so far as faith always exists in a specific self-understanding and is therefore bound up with specific conceptions of faith. From this standpoint, too, the history of faith certainly knows change, not only in the sense of the vicissitudes of decadence and reformation in the history of the church, but also in relation to Scripture itself. It would be a misunderstanding of the historicity of the history of faith to explain the Bible as the definitive and normative form of *conceptions* of faith. Admittedly, it would be difficult for anyone to risk the assertion—and not from formal respect for the authority of the Bible, but from an understanding of objective authority—that in relation to faith itself there has been any advance over the New Testament. No one will adopt such a naïve view of progress as to maintain that in the course of the history of the church faith has appeared in a truer and purer form than in the New Testament. And yet one can say that the history of faith in the history of the church has established knowledge about faith which cannot be cancelled, and one may even say authoritative experience. I mention just three outstanding examples.

First, the Christians of the first three centuries learned to perceive the mission of the faith to the world in dimensions which are scarcely mentioned in the New Testament, at any rate directly, namely, in the direction of responsibility for civilisation and the State. I need scarcely say that I am conscious of the questionable side of this development. But I must acknowledge that we can see in it a proper development of what the New Testament says of faith.

Second, the Reformation. It regarded itself simply as an exposition of Scripture. I do not wish to contest this. But what does it mean? At any rate, it does not exclude the expression, in this exposition, of the concern of faith in a sharper and more experiential fashion, so that our reading of the Bible would be the poorer if we had to do without the Reformation witnesses.

A third example, in my opinion, is the revolution which heralded the modern age. For a theological appraisal of this revolution much work has still to be done, and for a correct appraisal Reformation theology is still the best preparation. What kind of new beginnings may be said to be contained in this revolution which provide a further understanding of faith? The answer is connected with the new temptation which has appeared in the modern world. It could be described by different symptoms —the changed picture of the world, the collapse of the traditional metaphysic, the emergence of man taking over the world as a whole as his own responsibility, the secularisation which invades every sphere of life, and much besides. But this should all be seen as comprehended in the importance which history has for modern man. As we face this situation it looks as though we could advance a step in the objective exposition of what the New Testament calls faith, by recognising, that is to say, how faith, instead of being a turning away from history, opens up true freedom for history.

Since, as I have said, everything that is still to be said about faith concerns at heart the history of faith, we shall again and again have to deal with what I have just mentioned, the freedom for history that is opened up in faith.

III

The Record of Faith

If we ask what the nature of Christian faith is, we find we have to deal with history. Faith and history belong together. Moreover, my last lecture may have already indicated that faith and history are interwoven in a manifold and even confusing manner. Faith is dependent on tradition. For faith, we said, approaches us out of history, and takes us into its history. Admittedly, it takes us into a very ambiguous history, a history of deformations and transformations, though also of reformations, which also, however, bring about transformations, in which faith is forced into historical change. But this apparent threat to faith points to something very positive: faith discloses true freedom for history. On the one hand, therefore, faith is forced into historical change, in the world and the spirit and language. On the other hand, faith is forced to, or rather, itself urges on, a historical movement, a being on the way, to fulfil its existence in the affirmation of freedom. But of this we must speak later.

At present we are concerned with the one question: what have we to hold on to, in view of what we have said about the "history of faith," which can give us a clear and reliable picture of the nature of Christian faith? We can certainly not ignore all that the "history of faith" implies. But we need some firm foothold, if we are not to drift aimlessly on a wide sea. What are our criteria for separating the inessential and even the wrong from the nature of Christian faith? We said that faith is dependent upon tradition. Therefore we shall have to hold fast to the tradition of faith. But what is the authentic form in which this tradition reaches us? Can one not simply say, in the present-day message of the church? But which message, which church? It is a dilemma, but perhaps also a blessing, of the division of faith in Christendom that the question about the nature of Christian faith cannot be answered by pointing to the present results of the process of tradition. But rather this question compels us to critical questioning of the traditional answers.

But however much the traditional answers may contradict one another, even about what they consider to be the standard and norm, yet they are at one in ascribing unique authority to the Bible for answering the question about the nature of Christian faith. There is no Christian Church which does not acknowledge in principle this authority of the Bible. The differences arise only in the understanding and application of this authority. Moreover, the unanimity goes still further. However different, even opposed, the way in which the Bible is used, there is fundamental agreement that the decisive thing in the Bible is the witness to Christ, that is, the presentation of that which faith must hold to, since in fact as Christian faith it is faith in Jesus Christ. For however opposed the views which arise on this basis, nevertheless there is fundamental unity on this point, that faith, precisely defined, is not faith in the Bible but faith in Christ. As faith in Christ it is dependent on the tradition about Christ and hence upon the Bible. If faith is essentially faith in Christ, if therefore the nature of faith consists in the relation to Christ, then clearly the part played by the Bible as an authority must be more closely defined, if we are not to fall short of the decisive point.

The simplest and apparently self-evident interpretation of the authority of the Bible relates to its normative character. Scripture is regarded as a prescription, as regulations. But even if this view were allowed to stand, we should have to say that it does not go far enough. For the significance of a norm lies in its setting limits, which determine deviations to the right or the left or even give warning about them in advance. But the existence of what is thus kept within the norm is not a product of the norm. Life can be contained in regulations, but it cannot be brought about by them. In the form of a work of art certain laws can be recognised which then acquire normative significance. But a work of art does not arise from the mere following of such laws. Admittedly, this is not an entirely unobjectionable comparison, when we are considering the matter of faith. But there is without doubt one thing in common, that with faith, too, there may be norms and laws—whether it is a good thing to talk in this way is an open question—but norms and laws do not make faith. Hence it would in any case be insufficient to understand Holy Scripture to have authority merely in this normative sense. This would miss the most important thing about it. Scripture bears witness, in its witness to Christ, primarily to that on which faith lives, namely, the creative power which summons faith out of unbelief as it summons being out of non-being and light out of darkness. Primarily, therefore, authority must here be understood in the sense of authorship or originating power. And even if it is questionable whether one may simply ascribe to Holy Scripture itself this *auctoritas fidei*, this originating power of faith, the reference to the Bible certainly means something different from a mere reference to the authoritative norm. For to understand it in this way would mean that the Bible would only be consulted in cases of doubt, as a judicial instrument. But the real locus of the Bible is not where faith is being judged, but where it is being produced. Properly understood, the Bible is not a document of law, but a document of preaching. So if our question is, what must we cling to in order to have a clear and reliable knowledge of what Christian faith is, then we must see that this question cannot be separated from the question of how faith arises. And we find that we are referred to the Bible, which gives its real answer not as a document of law describing the nature of faith in a normative fashion, nor as a historical source-book telling us how and what was once believed, but as a document of preaching, to which the present-day witness of faith can appeal and by whose words faith can be kindled and nourished.

Although I have spoken of agreement among all Christian confessions in affirming the paramount authority of Scripture and recognising in the witness to Christ the heart of Scripture, it is clear that the proper understanding of this verbal agreement is hotly disputed. As is well known, the Reformed tradition takes the blunt instrument of the very wide and vague agreement, which leaves plenty of room for disagreement, and makes of it a sharp weapon: it speaks in accents of absoluteness and exclusiveness of *sola scriptura*, Scripture alone. The so-called Reformed principle of Scripture sounds quite unambiguous, but in fact it contains considerable problems. If they are not soberly faced, these suppressed problems can weigh heavily on the Protestant view of faith. Instead of being a service to faith, this so-called principle of Scripture can become a snare. The particle "alone" can only be properly understood when one knows what is meant to be excluded, and in what respect. It would be nonsensical to regard the Reformation slogan "through faith alone" as excluding works altogether. Works are only excluded from that on which before God I may depend. Similarly it would be nonsensical to regard the Reformation slogan of " Scripture alone " as allowing, say, the minister to give up reading theology with a good conscience, or as forbidding the pious Christian to read any other literature, on pain of a bad conscience. Rather the principle of Scripture is intended simply to exclude, but to exclude absolutely, any other witness in the matter of faith as binding save that which appeals to Scripture and submits to its scrutiny.

From the historical point of view this position is directed

against the Roman Catholic solution of the problem of authority. The intention of the latter had of course not been to diminish the authority of Scripture. If this were suspected a discussion with the Roman Catholics would be very difficult. For they of course maintain that nothing which contradicts Holy Scripture, or which is not found in it at least in embryo, is permissible in the church. There is a twofold justification for setting the authority of tradition alongside that of Scripture. First, the oral tradition has an interpretative character. For without some guiding line the Bible cannot be rightly understood, or at least it is liable to be misused. That is why the church, to which the Holy Spirit is promised and given, has both the right and the duty, for the sake of a right understanding of Scripture, to make binding decisions of interpretation, not, indeed, about every detail, but certainly about the most important questions, a decision about which gives a dogmatic definition to the understanding of Scripture in a specific historical situation. Second, the oral tradition has a complementary character, even though this cannot be sharply distinguished from the interpretative function. For not everything which was delivered by Jesus to the apostles was fixed in writing. And even if the existence of such traditions cannot be traced back to the very earliest times, it is to-day a kind of postulate of faith that even a view which emerged only later in the church's consciousness of its faith, if it meets with general approval and finally with confirmation from the infallible ecclesiastical doctrinal authority, was contained from the beginning in the tradition. The development of the mariological dogma in modern times is a familiar example of this procedure. Finally, in this precedence of tradition over Scripture and in the modern church as the criterion of tradition, we have an imposing solution of the problem of how the church, despite its bonds with its origin, can have room for historical development. However, we shall not discuss this Roman Catholic view of tradition at the moment, but shall go into some questions which concern directly the Reformation principle of Scripture.

From the Roman Catholic side the reproach has been levelled against the Reformation principle of Scripture—and not without some justification—of self-contradiction. For the acknowledgment of the canon of Holy Scripture in its traditional limits means the acknowledgment, in the absolute validity of Scripture, of the absolute validity of a decision of the early church. The principle of Scripture is therefore based, without its being admitted, on the Roman Catholic principle of tradition. This Roman Catholic objection of course does not contest that in Scripture—as of course the Reformers taught—we have to do with the Word of God. Nor is it contested that the biblical writings came into being in a different way from other literature, namely, by the inspiration of the Holy Spirit—a view which, indeed, very few biblical writings express about themselves, but which was a late Jewish view, taken over by the church along with the Old Testament, and later extended to the New Testament, while it was in process of formation. This view of inspiration was, and is to this day, undisputed in the Roman Catholic Church. But it was in Protestantism, not with the Reformers but in Old Protestant orthodoxy, that this view of inspiration was sharpened into the doctrine of verbal inspiration, in which not just each individual word but even the pointing of the Hebrew consonants—which has been proved to be a relatively late help in the reading inserted by the scribes—were declared to be directly inspired by the Holy Spirit and thus inerrant. Even if we admit that the special and unique nature of Holy Scripture is indicated by this view, Scripture cannot stand by itself in this way. The fact that these writings, and no others, compose the canon of Holy Scripture is not asserted by the writings themselves, but it is a judgment of the church which went through a long history before reaching a definitive expression.

The canonical status of New Testament writings such as the Second Epistle of Peter or the Epistle of Jude, the Book of Revelation and the Epistle to the Hebrews, and even the Gospel according to St. John, was disputed for a longer or shorter time, just as in the oldest canonical lists writings were named which did not in the end attain canonical status. By and large, one can say that the New Testament canon was formed about the year 200, but it was not until the fourth century that certain details were decided, while peripheral questions were being discussed long after that time. So far as the Old Testament canon is concerned, the church accepted the decision of late Jewish tradition, even receiving the somewhat broader canon of the Greek translation of the Old Testament, the so-called Septuagint. The Roman Catholic maintains this canon to this day, while the Reformers returned to the somewhat narrower canon of the Hebrew Bible. It is not possible to follow the history of the canon in detail. What matters for our argument is the basic fact that we are looking at two distinct events, first, the origin of the individual biblical writings, and second, their inclusion, grouping and reception as canonical writings. Even though it must be said that in respect of the latter event the church did not make sudden or arbitrary decisions, but accepted what had gradually won through and had created a status for itself, in other words, simply acknowledged the facts, yet it is beyond dispute that the closing of the canon was a decision, even, one might say, an act of confession, by the church.

If it is said that the Reformation principle of Scripture is in strange contradiction to this history of the formation of the canon, then we can only say—apparently surrendering this principle—all that the history of the canon makes clear is that its actual formation was by no means an infallible and irrevocable decision. If this sounds shocking, it should be recalled that Luther, on the basis of theological responsibility, was very free with the canon.

He not only questioned the canonicity of individual New Testament writings, such as the Book of Revelation and the Epistle of James, but in his translation of the New Testament he changed the order of some of the concluding writings, and left some of them out of the continuous numbering of the canonical books. To dispute the possibility of a revision of the canon is not a Protestant way of regarding the Bible. On the other hand, to be over-zealous for the necessity of a revision of the canon is also not a Protestant way of regarding the Bible. For quite apart from the fact that there is no single authority in Protestantism competent to make such a decision, and the further fact that the ancient delimitation of the canon must be on the whole described as astonishingly to the point, it betrays a totally misguided and in principle unfulfillable demand for guarantees of security, and indeed a totally misguided view of the nature of Holy Scripture, to wish to exclude the qualifications and contingencies of history. Such an effort would produce the illusory perfection of a bible so perfect that it required no more exposition.

Such an illusion about the Bible indicates a complete misunderstanding of what the Word of God means. We have just discussed the Reformed principle of Scripture in the light of the Roman Catholic objection. We must now set it clearly in opposition to a predominantly intra-Protestant misunderstanding, namely, the biblicist view. It is wrong to suppose that the so-called principle of Scripture is a purely Reformation insight. Medieval sects such as the Waldensians also opposed the Roman view of authority with a kind of principle of Scripture, when they allowed validity only to what is written in the Bible. But this is not evangelical doctrine in the Reformed sense. Rather, such a biblicism is usually at the service of a very un-Protestant legalism, in which absolute authority is accorded to individual Bible passages in isolation from the whole. This view is controlled by a positivist conception of revelation.

In biblicism contradictory tendencies are again and again violently united. On the one hand, there is the emphasis on the undiscriminated authority of the whole of Scripture. On the other hand, there is the arbitrary selection of individual passages as the shibboleth of true belief, specific moral demands or specific apocalyptic conceptions. The principle for understanding such passages is that of a strict literalism. On the other hand, everything which does not suit these views is interpreted allegorically, and with great freedom. Scripture is atomised into innumerable independent words of God, instead of being searched at every point for its relation to the one Word of God. In this multiplication the Word of God is simply law, and faith, too, is dissected into so many paragraphs of the divine law. Admittedly, immense pains are taken in the assimilation of Scripture. But the problem of its exposition, which must include the question of Scripture as a totality, is left untouched. The biblicist thinks that he is doing justice to Scripture if he adapts himself to the period from which it comes, if, for example, he tries to realise early Christianity as a timeless ideal, instead of letting Scripture encounter him where he is really living.

So we may see how in the problem of biblicism, as in that of the canon, the so-called Reformed principle of Scripture necessarily involves the task of exposition. This task has an importance which is unprecedented in the history of the church.

Of course, infinite pains have at all times been taken with the exposition of Scripture. Just as no other book has had a circulation in the least comparable to that of the Bible, nor been translated into so many languages (well over a thousand to-day), so too, no other book has produced such an immense literature or such a system of minute analysis. It is not only the difficult passages which pose a problem of exegesis. But also passages which are in themselves quite unambiguous, but which caused offence or seemed unedifying, have released a flood of exegetical efforts.

Such passages, indeed, were frequently preferred as objects of the art of exegesis. But one essential reason why the Bible has always demanded such an effort of interpretation is the astonishing and stimulating uniting of the Old and New Testaments in a double canon. This sets the question of the unity which is in the tension, and has again and again been a main drive in biblical exposition. But above all, the impulse to exposition arose from the power of the message itself with which the Bible is concerned, and which demands translation not only into other languages but also into other ages, other ways of thinking, other spiritual situations. Since something is here being said which emerges from historical distance to strike into the heart of our life, it is not possible, when understanding is not immediate, to rest content with the superficial recognition of that distance. But we must explore the depths, until what seems to have only a historical explanation really penetrates present-day understanding.

Although all those motifs were always at work, it was with the Reformation that something new took place in relation to the Bible, which lent to its interpretation an unheard-of urgency and seriousness. It is not enough to see only a quantitative increase of interest. But there is something qualitatively new, which I should in simplified terms describe as a *critical* exposition of Scripture.

First, it is critical in contrast with the traditional view, which held fast to certain dogmatic essentials, but within these limits left room for arbitrary and fantastic exegesis. In ecclesiastical usage the Bible was so domesticated that it could not become a danger to the ecclesiastical system, while among heretics, though it occasioned all kinds of revolutions, these were like summer lightning, touching only single points, superficially, and never breaking the spell of the basic traditional view. But in the Reformation the Bible began to be critical at a deep level of the traditional view of Christian faith, bringing about an upheaval from the very foundations. This was only apparently destructive and revolutionary, in reality it was constructive from within, and thus in sovereign fashion simply let the old view collapse. For it was on the basis of a new total understanding of faith that the all-transforming critical effects of Scriptural exposition penetrated the farthest regions of the church and the world. Never before or after has the world been changed to such an extent by exposition of Scripture.

But second, the exposition of Scripture was also critical of the dominant indiscipline of method. This is a sharp judgment. But it is justified, if one considers the great hermeneutic revolution, that is, the change in the method of interpreting Scripture, which was introduced by the Reformation. But what is most stirring is that the exegesis of Scripture became critical of Scripture itself. If our opponents play Scripture against Christ, Luther could say, then we play Christ against Scripture. His well-known judgment on the Epistle of James as an epistle of straw, because Christ is not its subject, was not a casual idea, but casts a vivid light on the scene: one must allow the individual passage of Scripture to say what it says, but one cannot simply assert that it is the Word of God. For the Word of God is solely that which proclaims and communicates the will of God as revealed in the crucified Christ.

For a long time no one had dared to criticise the actual content of the Bible openly, but only in a veiled fashion. The far-reaching consequences for method of Luther's revolutionary exegesis in the light of the clarity of Scripture were not realised, even in the Reformation. To the naïve observer the Reformed exegetical method is merely a new style of biblicism or dogmatism which then faced the great crisis brought about by the impact of historical and critical thought, an impact which seemed to force the whole traditional exegesis of Scripture into a hopeless position. For after the Reformation, with the aid of Scripture, had dethroned every authority, and ascribed all authority to the Bible alone, the Bible itself seemed to be overtaken in turn by the same fate of a twilight of the gods. The hidden ways in which it had come into being were now recognised, and they were at least in part quite other than the traditionally accepted view and than the assertions of the Bible itself. The impression of a unified presentation was broken, on close examination, into different literary layers. The dates of origin were often changed. The names of the authors were often shown to be pseudonyms. For instance, the second part of the Book of Isaiah is not by Isaiah at all; the Gospel according to St. John is in all probability not by John the son of Zebedee; not all the letters ascribed to St. Paul are genuinely Pauline; and so on. The assessment of the history of Israel underwent important changes. The course of early Christian history is incomparably more complicated than naïve acceptance of the New Testament would give us to suppose. And above all, many gaps have been disclosed in our historical knowledge of biblical events. Processes in tradition are now seen at work, which have transformed the original telling; legendary formations and mythological elements are now recognised.

This change in the understanding of the Bible is an occasion not for panic, but for thankfulness.

For first, although in individual points critical research may make mistakes which have to be corrected, on the whole this is a way of sober, conscientious recognition of the historical reality of the Bible. It makes the Bible more concrete. In any case, it is not right to fear the truth, however and wherever it comes to light.

Secondly, the historical and critical exegesis of the Bible, though separated by complicated cultural developments from the Reformation, is nevertheless inwardly connected to it. This exegesis compels us to follow into its theological depths the hermeneutic problem which was not fully thought out in the Reformation. In doing this it shows the correctness of the Reformation position, namely, that in its origin and structure

42

Scripture aims at preaching, it is a collection of kerygmatic writing, witnesses of faith.

Lastly, if a document is a valid record of a specific event, this concept fits both the Old and the New Testament in their difference and their unity. The Bible is the record of faith (and therefore also of unbelief), of the history of its expectation, its coming and its basic testimony.

IV

The Witness of Faith

Why do we come now to speak of Jesus? Why so soon? For if in the series of subjects within our main theme I am to follow a definite epistemological path, and also to respect, as a teacher should, the stages of difficulty, then it seems as though we were now being asked to take, instead of the next step, a mighty leap; to confront, not a preparatory and partial aspect, but the centre and thus the whole. For from all that we know of Christian faith, the difficult hurdle is what we are here asked to take, namely, to believe all that the Christian teaching has to say about Jesus Christ. One could also appeal to the series of themes in the Apostles' Creed. Is it advisable to discuss so soon those affirmations of faith which are to be found in the second article of the Creed, about Jesus Christ, and which are the most difficult of all to accept? Should we not first speak of faith in God, which can certainly not be presupposed as self-evident?

Now it is certainly not our purpose to build up a dogmatic system. Our purpose is much more elementary. We were trying to discover where and how faith occurs. That is why we began with the history of faith. Then we found ourselves led to Scripture as the record of faith. Whatever unclarities remain, in one respect we have been given a clear and indisputable answer to the question about the nature of Christian faith: faith knows that it is dependent upon Jesus Christ, and confesses therefore that it is faith in Jesus Christ. This is the unambiguous witness of the history of the church, however much controversy there may be about the interpretation of this basic confession. This is also the unambiguous view of the New Testament. And even if it is doubtful what the relation of the Old Testament is to this witness to Christ, it is clear that the acceptance of the Old Testament by Christianity rests upon the conviction that it falls in with the witness to Christ. We are therefore following the most elementary indication of Christian faith when we now turn to Jesus Christ.

The question how this is to happen shows in another respect the connection between this theme and the previous one. The close connection of faith and history was, as we saw, somewhat disturbing. In our discussion of the Bible, especially in our remarks about the historical and critical standpoint, this disturbing factor became really explosive. But the discussion was too brief to make clear what was happening, let alone to settle the matter. But we cannot escape this problem. For when we now ask about Jesus, we have to deal with the phenomenon of historical criticism in its extreme sharpness. In the whole realm of historical investigation there is no more instructive example of the problem of the historical-critical method than the question of the historical Jesus. And within theology there is no point at which the question set by historical criticism has a more agitating effect. What is the relation of the historical Jesus to the Christ of faith?

The very name Jesus Christ, a double name, fixes the point which we must inquire into. Jesus, the man who lived in Palestine nearly two thousand years ago; and Christ, the title of honour by which faith confesses him as present Lord and Saviour. So it is not really a double name but the primitive form of the Christian confession of faith, Jesus the Christ. This means that Jesus and faith are joined together as closely as possible; first, in that faith is dependent on Jesus, it is faith *in* him; and second, clearly, in that this Jesus is to a certain extent dependent on faith: only faith can recognise him as he wishes to be recognised.

Here the critical question arises, whether faith in Jesus has any support in the historical Jesus himself? And what support does the historical Jesus offer for faith in him? These questions are not asked maliciously, from outside. The Christian message itself keeps these questions alive. It sets decisive weight upon the assertion that Jesus is not a mythical but a historical figure. If Jesus had never lived, or if faith in him were shown to be a misunderstanding of the significance of the historical Jesus, then clearly the ground would be taken from under Christian faith. If it lost its support in the historical Jesus, it would perhaps not be simply devoid of an object, but it would lose the object which has always been proclaimed by Christianity as the central object of faith.

The way in which the man Jesus is proclaimed as the object of faith makes great difficulties when we try to make this historical human life of Jesus tally with what faith says of it. For apparently we are being asked to hold as true of a real man something that contradicts all experience of real human life, to acknowledge as a historical event something that we could not accept as historical in any other account. I am not thinking at the moment of the miracle stories, which constitute no small part of the tradition. The decisive offence comes with the assertion which has always been central to faith in Christ, namely, that after his crucifixion he rose again from the dead on the third day and that his life reached its goal and conclusion, or rather, eternal duration by his ascension into heaven. And as the historical account here goes beyond death, contradicting the nature of a historical account, it also claims to be able to give an account of life before birth, thus here too overstepping the bounds of a historical account. If Christian dogma sets the words "true God" alongside the words "true man," then despite all assurances that both descriptions hold good, unmingled, it is unclear how this can still be a real man. Hence the impression made by the dogmatic picture of Christ is that of a heavenly being in human form, but not that of a man of flesh and blood like ourselves. If it did not sound so shocking, one would be inclined to say that after all we have to do with a mythical and not a historical manifestation—or at least with a historical figure in mythical trappings.

But the traditional dogmatic image of Christ does not only call in question the real human life of Jesus—I repeat, in spite of all assurances to the contrary; but it also calls in question the very aim of that dogmatic image, namely, faith in Christ. For this most significant of all objects of faith becomes, at least for many, the greatest hindrance to faith. How often can we hear—and how much more often is the complaint not uttered—that someone cannot accept Christian faith because he cannot believe the alleged historical facts about Jesus. And he who can bring himself, or at least force himself, to believe these things, seems after all to reflect a distorted image of faith, as an achievement of his own, as a law that he must take on himself in addition to everything else, as believing the incredible, as taking to be historical something that he cannot with a good conscience so understand.

If this were the actual state of affairs, the results for Christian faith would be catastrophic. But according to St. Paul faith is not bondage to the law, but freedom from the law. And according to the witness of the whole New Testament Jesus is not an awkward object of faith, but the source of faith; he does not make faith harder, but he makes it possible.

A sense of the contradiction in this view of faith, together with an increasing lack of understanding for the nature of assertions of faith, and with a candid and untraditional approach to history, combined, at the beginning of modern times, to produce the attempt at a portrait of the historical Jesus independent of the dogmatic portrait of Christ. This has sometimes resulted in a clinging, not to the Christ of faith, but to the man Jesus in his natural humanity, as this can be reconstructed from the pictures touched up by later piety. In such a case the transition from the preaching Jesus to the preached Christ was regarded as a dubious matter, indeed, as a complete misunderstanding of what Jesus wished. To put it in slogans, we must go back from the heavenly Lord to the teacher and model, back from the time after Easter to the time before Easter, or simply, back from Paul (who is regarded as the founder of traditional Christianity) to Jesus himself, from a Christianity of difficult credal statements to a Christianity of simple trust in God and of practical love.

This movement was twofold: first it used the tools of criticism in order to demolish the dogmatic tradition, replacing it by more comprehensible religious ideas, of which Jesus was regarded as the representative; and second, it worked at the historical reconstruction of the real life of Jesus. Albert Schweitzer's most significant theological work is his critical survey of this research into the life of Jesus, a process which went on for more than two hundred years (*The Quest of the Historical Jesus*). The result is paradoxical and can cause as much bewilderment on the historical way to Jesus as on the dogmatic way. The constantly changing portrayals of the life of Jesus were shown by Schweitzer to be largely dogmatic, only not dogmatic in the traditional way, and moreover very uncritical combinations of the traditional material. They used the methods of the psychologist and the novelist to fill in the gaps and to give form to the apparently arbitrary traditional material. Moreover, close examination brought to light certain strange traits which did not suit the desired portrait of Jesus. Lastly, it was recognised that the whole enterprise was bound to fail because even the oldest traditional material is determined by faith in Jesus, and therefore does not convey a neutral historical picture. Scholars went out to seek Jesus, and ended once again with the primitive witness to Christ as the ultimate attainable authority. The consequence was embarrassment at the disappearance of the "historical" Jesus, or resolute renunciation of any historical quest of Jesus himself behind the proclamation, or finally (among the defenders of the old dogmatic tradition and the opponents of the return to the mere historical Jesus), horror at the thought that the alleged historical foundation for their dogmatic Christ was called in question.

In order to reach a proper judgment about this situation, we must give at least a cursory glance at the source material. We know of Jesus only from the Christian tradition, which has been determined by faith. References in classical authors or in rabbinic tradition are secondary, scarce and unrewarding. At most they are useful as witnesses for dispelling any doubt that Jesus really lived. But what is noteworthy is that, apart from the Gospels, the primitive Christian writings provide only meagre historical references to the life of Jesus. The Pauline letters do not mention much more about the historical Jesus than the facts of his birth and crucifixion, the description of his way as obedience, and, in addition, a few of his sayings. These sayings, moreover, apart from the words of institution of the Lord's Supper, are not particularly important, nor do they have a prominent place in the Pauline gospel. On careful examination some concealed relationships may be discovered, and it may also be assumed that Paul knew more of Jesus than he discloses in his epistles. Nevertheless, the impression remains that however important the manifestation of Jesus was for him, the biographical detail was unimportant.

In the Gospels, however, things are different. But here too the material is strange. Even as a literary genre the Gospels are unique. In classical literature comparisons could at most be sought in historical and biographical literature. But these show only that the Gospels have no model. Their purpose is simply and solely the proclamation of the message. This explains why the early church was not embarrassed about putting four Gospels side by side in the canon. One of these, the Gospel according to John, traces such a strange and independent path for itself, in comparison with the other, older Gospels that a historical account in the strict sense is not expected of it. The other three Gospels, on the other hand, display so much agreement with one another that they call for a comparative, synoptic examination (hence they are called the "synoptic" Gospels). But this means that they confront the reader with all their differences and contradictions, which cannot decently be harmonised. When they are considered as witnesses to faith, this diversity need not be a disturbance. But as soon as a historical question is asked, critical operations are essential. If anyone is annoyed by such critical work, let him take some example himself, say the parable of the invitation to the wedding-feast (Matthew 22.1-14, Luke 14.16-24); but let him not produce the lame conclusion that Jesus told the parable twice, once in Matthew's way, and the other time in Luke's way.

The study of the Synoptic Gospels has from the standpoint of literary criticism reached an almost universally agreed result. Mark is the oldest Gospel. Besides Mark there existed a collection (no longer extant) of the sayings of Jesus. Matthew and Luke, independently of one another, made use of both sources, in addition to special material of their own. The Synoptic Gospels were completed, as literary entities, in a space of approximately forty to sixty years after the death of Jesus. They are therefore not so old as the Pauline Epistles, which are far and away the oldest New Testament writings. Nevertheless, the evangelists made use of material, some of which had a long history, both written and oral. A comparison of the Synoptic Gospels casts direct light on the written phase of the tradition, so-called form criticism casts indirect light on the preceding oral tradition. Every reader of the

Gospels knows how they are composed of tiny units, whose significance lies in themselves, and whose connections are secondary—for example, miracle stories, controversies, parables, separate sayings. These units had first of all a long oral tradition, in which they possibly underwent changes as the result of certain tendencies, which explains certain new formations. For every living piece of tradition has what is called its sociologically determined "*Sitz im Leben*" or place in life, and this place gives it its specific character. The Synoptic tradition must therefore in the first instance be interpreted from the standpoint of this question: to what extent did the living carrier of this tradition, early Christianity, influence the formation of the material?

Here it is only possible to outline some conclusions. The chronological biographical framework into which the evangelists fitted the traditional material is their own composition, and reveals certain theological intentions. It is only the scenes from the last days of Jesus' life which have a connected context, which is certainly very old. This is a sign of how the death of Jesus became to some extent the point of crystallisation for the tradition. The stories of the childhood, on the other hand, are late and legendary formations. The tendency at work in them is continued and intensified in the apocryphal gospels (that is, those which have not been accepted as canonical). In the stories of the Gospels, moreover, as well as in the conversations, we must reckon with the powerful formative influence of the early Christian tradition. For what those early Christians knew of the life of Jesus they saw, understandably enough, in the light of their faith in him. Handing down a tradition became interpretation, and interpretation was stylised, not merely in a literary but also in a historical sense. For the aim was not to communicate who Jesus had been, and how he had once been regarded, but who Jesus is and how he may now be understood in faith. It is Luke who first begins to combine with his intention a quasi-historical interest. It is therefore not easy to know in each individual instance where we are dealing with authentic material in the historical sense. In the sayings and conversations, generally speaking, there is greater historical faithfulness than in the stories. Wherever provenance from the Jewish world or from early Christian ideas is out of the question, we are in all probability dealing with a historically faithful tradition about Jesus. In this situation it cannot surprise us that we cannot elicit from the sources what as witnesses of faith they have no desire to mediate, namely, a biography of Jesus which is chronologically coherent and psychologically transparent. On the contrary, we must be surprised at the fact that despite all the difficulties we do gain a historically reliable general impression of Jesus.

If we attempt to reach a synoptic view, we do well to begin with the words of Jesus.

The rule of God is undoubtedly the core of his message. This thought has deep roots in the Old Testament. With the help of the Psalms, above all, it is possible to reconstruct the annual celebration of a festival in which Jahweh ascends the throne—not in the sense of celebrating the foundation of the kingdom, as something that is past and is now being commemorated, but in the sense of an ever new proclamation of something that is actually happening. For on the Old Testament view to speak of the rule of God always means to speak of his coming. For God's coming is the way in which God prevails. This essential point in the Old Testament understanding of God was separated off, in late Judaism, from the present, and became something that was expected in the future. In this sense the coming rule of God was spoken of in different ways: among the Zealots from the political aspect, as a national hope for the future, and in apocalyptic writings from the cosmological aspect of world history, as an expectation for the general future. Jesus' message of the imminence of the rule of God is sharply divided from the hope of the Zealots. Comparatively speaking, it is nearer to the apocalyptic expectation, but is unmistakably distinct from it as well, by its rejection of any interest in an apocalyptic chronology of the end, as well as by its renunciation of any fantasies about the future. In contrast to this it has been said that the peculiarity of the message of Jesus is in its announcement of the immediate temporal nearness of the rule of God. This view has without doubt an element of truth. Even in John the Baptist this expectation of the immediate nearness of the rule of God played a part; and it may be taken as certain that Jesus permitted himself to be baptized by John, and followed in his footsteps. In the Gospels we find words which express unambiguously this expectation of the end: " Truly I say unto you, among those who stand here are some who shall not taste death till they have seen the kingdom of God come with power " (Mark 9.1). Albert Schweitzer and others, in healthy reaction against an all too familiar portrait of Jesus, have emphasised the historical strangeness which Jesus has for us, on account of this unfulfilled and unrepeatable expectation of the end. But here, too, there has been a one-sided emphasis on what seemed to be the essential thing. There have been many Messianic pretenders. And we know from the recently discovered Qumran texts how strong was the expectation of the end in which the Jewish sect lived which inspired them. This kind of thing was in the air. And it is worthy of note that it is at least very uncertain whether in his proclamation of the imminent rule of God Jesus made an explicit Messianic claim at all, or even had any specific Messianic view.

The emphasis does not lie on a spectacular apocalyptic happening, but on the nearness of God himself. The essential thing in the nearness of the rule of God is the rule of the God who is near. And on my view what is peculiar and unique in Jesus' proclamation of the rule of God is that his call to repentance is wonderfully transformed into a call to joy. The message of Jesus does not aim at instilling fear, but at giving courage. And while to call God " Father " is not new, with Jesus it has decisive significance in its new expression. And if we ask what is special in the content of Jesus' words about the rule of God, then we must say that it lies in the encouraging announcement of what is about to meet us. The dominant note is the present attitude to what is already on the way. A man has discovered a hidden treasure. It would be stupid, he thinks, not to scrape together a little money in order to acquire the land where the treasure is. To rouse the sleepy is also part of this encouragement, for suddenly it may be too late. God can break in on us like a thief in the night. So take heart and be awake! The coming of God can also be unexpectedly long delayed. So take heart and be patient! But he who has reason for being afraid, like that prodigal fellow who has run away from his father, let him take heart just because his father is near. For he is awaited with joy. How many of the parables of Jesus end in joy! And they all represent an event in which in one way or the other we already participate. The concreteness of the parables is likewise a unique and unmistakable element in Jesus' proclamation of the kingdom of God. The form corresponds to the content. The imminence of the rule of God is expressed in the concrete language of every day. The mother kneading the dough in the kitchen, the farmer sowing the seed, provide the language for speaking of the rule of God: so near is God. And the parables of Jesus are even more concrete. Someone goes preaching through the land, to no purpose for many, but for some the words take root and bear fruit, as in the parable of the sower. A preacher of repentance sits down at table with sinners, like the father in the parable. " So it is with the kingdom of God," says the explanation. Can one avoid seeing what the nearness of the rule of God means? Should one not take heart at this nearness? And that means, should one not believe?

Closely connected with this message of the imminent rule of God is the message of the will of God. Jesus seemed to be a wandering rabbi. But a rabbi teaches that " Moses said." Jesus seemed to be a prophet. But a prophet usually says, " Thus saith the Lord." Jesus uses neither form in order to assert his authority. He uses the unprecedented words, " Verily I say unto you." This is typical of the enigmatic and extraordinary way in which he expounds the law; " he taught as one who had authority, and not as the scribes " (Matthew 7.29). But he did not reserve this sovereign freedom for himself as his prerogative. In his exposition of the law, it is true, he sharpens it to an infinite degree. The cure must begin, not where the sore gathers and bursts, but in the hidden seat of the impurity. Murder is accomplished in the heart, before it is accomplished by the hand—even without its ever being accomplished by the hand. This radical view means a liberation from all anxious or refined casuistry, a liberation to do the will of God. It also means a liberation in the sense of distinguishing between what is important and what is trivial, so that you do not strain out a gnat and swallow a camel. It is not a sign of freedom to be meticulous about rules of purity and not to know where the source of impurity is. It is not a sign of freedom to break the Sabbath in an emergency when an ox has fallen into a well, but to let your neighbour wait, whom you could help and give joy to, for the sake of what you call God's will. To be pious and be lacking in love, to maintain the law of God in principle and in general, but to ignore its concrete demands—these are no sign of freedom. The freedom which Jesus took for himself and which he gave to others, in full authority, are inextricably connected. He taught the will of God in such a way that we are impelled to say, Yes, this is how it is. We are given courage to believe, and that means, courage to be free.

The authority of Jesus reached its climax in the call to discipleship. This is something strange and unique, in contrast with this world around him. Rabbis had pupils, and revolutionaries had adherents. Jesus' call to discipleship could be misunderstood in both directions. But he asked neither for pupils nor for revolutionary action, but only that men should share in his way. Nor did he summon everyone to discipleship, though in the last resort he was speaking of something that concerned everyone: they were to let their way be determined, without anxiety, by the rule of the God who is near. The call to discipleship is in the last resort simply the call to faith. For faith cannot be more concretely expressed than by saying, Be not anxious, for the heavenly Father knows what we need.

These elements in the message of Jesus—the nearness of the rule of God, the clarity of his will, and the simplicity of discipleship, with joy, freedom, and lack of anxiety—are the interpretation of one thing, the call to faith. But it is all seen in the context of the remarkable authority of the Person of Jesus. If discipleship means sharing in the way of Jesus, then understanding his preaching of the will of God means sharing in his freedom, and understanding his message of the rule of God means sharing in his joy, his obedience, and his courage in face of the nearness of God.

What Jesus says cannot be separated from his Person, and his Person is one with his way. The way which he goes raises the question of what his words mean. And his words explain the meaning of his way. His way includes his community with tax-gatherers and sinners, and his healing of the sick. For it was as a witness of faith that he healed the sick, encouraging them to the faith that removes mountains, and saying to them, " Your faith has saved you." It includes above all going his way to the end; it includes holding fast the witness of faith, in face of the charge of blasphemy and sedition; it includes the affirmation of God's nearness in the dereliction on the Cross: "My God, my God, why hast thou forsaken me?" (Mark 15.34).

This was the end of the witness of faith. The Epistle to the Hebrews calls him "the pioneer and perfecter of faith" (Hebrews 12.2). With what right? This is our question as we turn to the Easter event and the birth of faith in Jesus Christ.

V

The Basis of Faith

We have now to discuss the question which follows directly from the last lecture. How did Jesus, the witness of faith, become the basis of faith? That is simply the precise formulation of the historical question: how did the transition take place from Jesus himself to the church's proclamation of Christ? The answer of the Christian tradition is quite specific and unanimous. At the point of transition is the resurrection of Jesus from the dead. However enigmatic this answer sounds to us, at least it means that there can be no talk of a direct continuation. Certainly there is a connection, but it is marked by abrupt discontinuity. And if nevertheless we can speak of a continuation, it can only be grasped as the act of God. The transition from the "historical Jesus" to the Christ of faith is no more a matter of course than is the leap from death to life.

This moment of discontinuity corresponds to the way in which the transition from Jesus to early Christianity is represented. The execution of Jesus and the flight of the disciples give a picture of such complete failure that it is, to say the least, an enigma that the very opposite of failure arises, namely, the insistent proclamation of Jesus Christ in the whole world. This cannot be simply derived from Jesus himself, as the carrying out of his programme and injunctions after his death, as a task for which the disciples had pulled themselves together after the initial shock. It is only at the Last Supper that Jesus seems to have given instructions which envisaged the time after his death, when, in the night in which he was betrayed, he said, " This do in remembrance of me" (I Corinthians 11.24f.). For everything else a new beginning is made. In the tradition itself it is clearly said that the mission to preach and baptize came not from the earthly Jesus but from the Resurrected One. Nor can we speak of a direct and explicit founding of the church by Jesus, nor of any teaching which Jesus gave concerning himself, which had simply to be spread abroad. And in fact the direct passing on of what Jesus himself taught played only a secondary part in the message of early Christianity. Nor would it have been susceptible of direct handing on. For Jesus' teaching was so united with his Person that it would have been difficult after his death to abstract a general collection of ideas as material for preaching, quite apart from the question whether his death did not have to be regarded as the refutation of his message concerning the nearness of the rule of God.

These signs of discontinuity, however, are opposed by signs of continuity. In early Christianity it was a matter of course that the risen Lord was identical with Jesus himself. The faith which now took hold of the disciples and which they bore witness to was faith in this Jesus. It is entirely to this primitive faith in Jesus that we owe the tradition about Jesus. And however dubious it may be how far this primitive faith in Jesus—and all the new elements which appeared along with it—could really appeal to Jesus, nevertheless, in one point there is an indisputable and decisive connection with Jesus, namely, that Jesus and faith are indissolubly connected. His message, his influence, his way, his whole life was a witness of faith which aimed at summoning to faith and at awakening faith. Even his death, his death above all, is part of this witness of faith. Jesus so devoted himself to this mission that his death was the extreme fulfilment of the witness of faith, and thus the summary of his life. To be committed to Jesus now meant to be committed to faith. Was Jesus, and with

him faith, simply extinguished? Or was it through death that
Jesus reached the goal as the witness of faith, so that the fire of
faith began to burn and to spread? In early Christianity it was
the latter which was affirmed, and affirmed by deeds. The faith
of early Christianity understood itself in terms of Jesus having
reached the goal, but exclusively in the form of testifying that
Jesus is risen.

It must simply be accepted as a fact that early Christianity saw
it in this way, and the proclamation of the church has from that
time gone on repeating that Christian faith stands and falls with
the witness to the resurrection of Jesus from the dead. St. Paul
never ceased to emphasise this: "If Christ has not been raised,
then our preaching is in vain and your faith is in vain. We are
even found to be misrepresenting God, because we testified of
God that he raised Christ, whom he did not raise if it is true that
the dead are not raised. If Christ has not been raised, your faith
is futile and you are still in your sins." (I Cor. 15.14ff.)

St. Paul does not mean, if the resurrection of Jesus is untenable,
then this one article of faith, faith in the resurrection of Jesus, is
untenable. But rather, faith as a whole would be finished. It
would be senseless. And this is the unanimous witness of the early
church. When Christian faith speaks about its basis, it points
with monotonous regularity to the crucified Jesus, of whom it is
known that he is risen. This Easter witness is the germ of the
Christian confession of faith, and has remained as its constitutive
core.

That the witness to the resurrection of Jesus has this significance
we must at least take notice of, as a historical fact. But this is
just what seems to one who is concerned with Christian faith to
be an oppressive burden. How is one meant to understand "risen
from the dead"? Is this not in fact for most Christians a hard
law of faith, to which faith must more or less resolutely submit,
but by which it does not live? Can we agree with a good con-

science with St. Paul, and draw the harsh consequence that if Christ is not risen then Christian proclamation and faith itself are meaningless? Do the words of the Creed, "the third day he rose again from the dead," not stand in a series of other similarly problematic assertions, such as those about the Virgin Birth, the Descent to Hell, and the Ascension? How can we simply swallow all this literally, or at any rate in the way a modern man thinks he has to understand it, with his urge to historical and physical objectification?

One important correction requires to be made straightaway. It is wrong to put all the clauses from the second article of the Apostles' Creed on the same level. At any rate, this is not in the least what we find in the primitive tradition. If we stick to the New Testament writings, we find that the Virgin Birth and the Descent to Hell are mentioned only in very few places, and without exception in late material. The same is true of the Ascension, so far as a separate event alongside the Resurrection is intended and not simply the Resurrection itself as the exaltation to the right hand of God. In the Christian year the span of forty days between Easter and Ascension is derived from a single reference by St. Luke, in the first chapter of Acts. The church later accepted this Lucan chronology, which now seems so much a matter of course. St. Paul mentions neither the Virgin Birth, nor the Descent to Hell, nor the Ascension, nor the scheme of the forty days.

But it is quite a different matter with the mention of the Resurrection of Jesus. If every reference were collected, we should have to write out a very large part of the New Testament. If the few remarks about the other ideas were not to be found in the New Testament, then nothing at all in Christian faith would be changed. But if the witness to the Resurrection were cut out, then the essence of Christian faith would be impaired. I cannot now enter upon a discussion of those isolated references of peripheral Christological utterances in the New Testament. But all the same it must be clearly said that to see these references as reports of historical events, and to shirk the admission that they are legendary and mythological conceptions, would be a sign that the New Testament is not being taken seriously. The testimony to the Resurrection of Jesus, on the other hand, is closely bound up in the source material with the testimony to specific historical events. And so far as Christian faith is in fact expressed in those peripheral utterances—and I have no wish to contest this—their meaning and validity are entirely dependent upon the confession of the Resurrection of Jesus. To make this distinction, and thus to concentrate everything on the question of the witness to Easter, is not an arbitrary choice, but is dictated by respect for the truth.

If we now turn to this particular question of the Resurrection of Jesus, we must guard against error by saying in advance three things. First, we must clearly recognise, what I have already suggested, that the Resurrection of Jesus is not to be regarded as one object of faith alongside others, as though Easter only added the Resurrection of Jesus as something to be believed along with everything else. Rather, faith in the Resurrected One simply expresses faith in Jesus. This is not something additional to the Person of Jesus, but Jesus himself. Second, we must keep in mind that, since we have to do with the Person of Jesus himself, we are not speaking of an *object* of faith, but about the witness of faith who becomes the basis of faith. When the Easter faith comes into being, what is new is not a new object of faith, but the coming into being, the being awakened and coming alive of faith itself. This may even be seen in the language, for now the idea of faith suddenly takes the centre of the stage in a quite new way, and undergoes creative linguistic changes. And this is not surprising, for as we have already hinted, in faith Jesus reaches his goal. Easter has clearly to do with the confession that Jesus has reached his goal. And lastly, he who is concerned with the nature of

Christian faith has every reason to show, at this point above all, perseverance and courage for the truth. It is unworthy of Jesus and of Christian faith to dodge the issue here, whether by making a *sacrificium intellectus* along with weighty assertions of what you do not understand, or by deceiving oneself and others by means of apologetic and dialectical tricks, or by making do with a phantom faith, in resigned or superficial mood. In my opinion the very existence of Christianity is at stake, in the way it answers this question: whether it repeats the confession of the risen Jesus half-heartedly and with a bad conscience, or whether it does it with conviction, joyfully and convincingly, finding itself at the source and basis of faith.

We must look again at the nature of the texts, and the layers of the tradition. It is impossible, in the limits at our disposal, to make a convincing study of the matter for one who is completely uninstructed. It is more likely that such an attempt would only do damage. But I trust the good sense of the ill-informed, and their readiness to be informed. I shall give a broad outline of what is generally agreed among responsible theologians, apart from individual modifications.

The New Testament references to the Resurrection of Jesus fall into three main groups. The first is the well-known Easter stories which are found in the closing chapters of the four Gospels. The second is composed of the formulas of proclamation or confession. The third is a single text, which really belongs to the second group, but for various reasons must be given a special place, namely, I Corinthians 15.3-8.

These three groups could be provisionally described as follows. The Easter stories of the four Gospels contain a great deal of concrete and individual detail. But if we try to combine them in a single historical account, we do violence to their nature and their meaning. In fact, this kind of harmonising is simply not possible. The synoptic comparison which is possible elsewhere with the first three Gospels breaks down here, as it does with the stories of Jesus' infancy. None of the accounts can be identified with another. We are dealing with traditional material, which, though certainly old, has been embellished at a relatively late period with legendary accretions, each account being independent of the others. I shall return to this later.

The second group consists of brief formulas having the character of testimony, which are variations of the pure assertion of the Resurrection of Jesus. In all this material there are no concrete details at all, whether about the tomb or about the appearances of the Resurrected Jesus. Not a word is said about these matters in this group of texts. Typical examples are Acts 2.24 and 3.15.

I Corinthians 15.3ff. is different, indeed unique. As it is so important I give it in full. St. Paul is writing to the Corinthians:

> " For I delivered to you as of first importance what I also received, that Christ died for our sins in accordance with the scriptures, that he was buried, that he was raised on the third day in accordance with the scriptures, and that he appeared to Cephas, then to the twelve. Then he appeared to more than five hundred brethren at one time, most of whom are still alive, though some have fallen asleep. Then he appeared to James, then to all the apostles. Last of all, as to one untimely born, he appeared also to me."

First, we may note that this text is very early, and of unquestioned authenticity. The First Epistle to the Corinthians was written in the year 56/57, that is, about 25 years after the death of Jesus. The chronology of this early period is admittedly not absolutely certain. Nevertheless, we can reach fairly exact results in our dating. The death of Jesus would be in the year 30 or 33, and the conversion of Paul between 33 and 35, that is, about three years after the death of Jesus. Now Paul, as he explicitly says, is quoting in I Corinthians 15 a tradition which he has received.

This therefore reaches back much earlier than the year 56. It cannot be decided, nor does it matter very much, whether Paul received this tradition at the time of his conversion or only later. What is of crucial importance is that this text takes us quite close to the event which it describes. And the mention of certain witnesses by name, who were still alive, made this tradition susceptible of control. Moreover, Paul knew the chief witnesses personally. It is therefore to be noted that the message of the Resurrection directs us not to some nebulous and distant mythical realm, but to a sharply circumscribed place in history.

Of course, not the whole text which I have quoted comes from that ancient tradition. Paul himself adds the reference at the end to his experience at Damascus. And stylistic criteria indicate with a fair measure of certainty that the mention of other appearances has been added to the basic material. In the original kernel four things are asserted: dead, buried, risen, appeared. These four fall into two groups; for "dead" and "risen" are documented respectively by "buried" and "appeared." This formula, which is concentrated on death and resurrection, comments on them with the aid of two brief quotations from Scripture. On death the comment is "for our sins," following Isaiah 53.5; and on resurrection the comment is "on the third day," following Hosea 6.2. Finally, Peter and the Twelve are named as the earliest witnesses of the Resurrection, that is, as those to whom the first appearances were vouchsafed. Nor may doubt be cast on the later evidences. Presumably they came to be added later because they took place after a certain space of time from the earliest appearances. If we take everything together, then what we learn seems to be meagre. There is nothing about the event of the Resurrection itself, except for the apparently exact description of the time, "on the third day." But like the words "for our sins" this is a quotation from Scripture, and it is at least questionable whether we may also take it as a piece of historical information. For how could this information have been given except by the first appearance? But the first appearance is undated. Indeed only the bare minimum is said of the appearances. We learn nothing about the manner of them, of the locality, but only the names of those who experienced them, together with a relative chronology. For the series undoubtedly indicates a temporal succession, stretching till the conversion of Paul, that is, somewhat over three years. It was obviously unnecessary to say more. The names of the witnesses and the testimony to the Resurrected One were enough.

If we now turn back, from these sparse, sober and reliable statements, to the richly embellished Easter stories of the Gospels, it is clear that in many regards pious imagination was at work. Admittedly the Gospels are restrained in comparison with the apocryphal Gospels, which went much further. Unlike the Gospel of Peter, the canonical Gospels do not depict the actual happening of the Resurrection. Nor was idle fantasy at work in the embellishment, but certain theological tendencies which aimed at proclaiming the message not by abstract statements but by concrete depiction. Thus, for example, we have all those motifs which contend with the suspicion that the body had been stolen, or those motifs which are opposed to a spiritualistic interpretation of the Resurrection.

The tradition of these Easter accounts went through a certain history which we are able to analyse, so that certain primal elements may be discerned. The starting-point for this analysis is provided by the following observation. Two types of stories are found in juxtaposition: stories of the tomb, and stories of appearances. In the course of the tradition these two types have drawn closer together and overlapped to some extent. But careful analysis shows two quite distinct types. The stories of the tomb testify to the Resurrection in a certain negative way, proceeding from the discovery that the tomb was empty. These stories were originally told only of the women who followed Jesus, not of the disciples. In these stories there was no appearance of Christ, but only angelic appearances. The stories of the appearances, on the other hand, had originally nothing to do with the locality of the tomb. They happen only to disciples, not to the women. And there is nothing in them about angels, but the Lord himself makes his appearance. If we add that according to Mark and Matthew the appearances took place in Galilee, and according to Luke and John (leaving aside the appendix of John 21) in Jerusalem, it is clear that we have a very complicated situation. It is obviously impossible to clarify every detail with certainty. But some things can be established with certainty, and others with a high degree of probability.

The whole of the rest of the tradition, including the Pauline, is silent about the empty tomb. We must not confuse the view which can result from certainty about the Resurrection, that as a consequence the tomb must be empty, with the experience which is here asserted, namely, that the tomb was, astonishingly, found to be empty. And if the fact of the empty tomb is never used as an argument, by St. Paul or anywhere else, and if even in that earliest tradition quoted in I Corinthians 15 there is nothing about the discovery of the empty tomb, then it appears that no significance was attached in the message of early Christianity to the fact, so far as the tradition of it was known at all. For there is no doubt that the early tradition of the Easter event consists of accounts of the appearances. The only certain things we know about them are what we learn from St. Paul. We cannot identify them with specific accounts in the Gospels. But with their help we may regard it as very probable that at least the first appearances took place in Galilee. For the disciples fled from Jerusalem, and only returned there after they believed. Later the happenings were varied and overlaid by different motives, just as the accounts of Mark and Matthew on the one hand, and those of Luke and John on the other, are mutually exclusive. It is probable that the accounts of the empty tomb are part of these late additions. If they should nevertheless possess a historical core, this does not make faith in the Risen One easier. For the empty tomb can also be interpreted in other ways—as indeed was done earlier. Faith in the Risen One must therefore be understood as binding us to a physiological conception of the Resurrection, or we must admit the possibility that the tomb was empty for other reasons, and that the discovery accidentally coincided with the appearances of the Risen One (to rule out other fantasies from the beginning). In that case one should have to believe in the Risen One *in spite of* the empty tomb, and without letting oneself be troubled by this enigmatic and ambiguous fact.

We have already reached the question how this witness to the Resurrection, with its undoubted historical core in various appearances, is to be understood. I must confine myself to a few points.

It is an early objection to the appearances of the Risen One, and one which was thoroughly exploited in antiquity, that they occurred not to neutral witnesses but to believers. More accurately, one must say that they occurred only to those who became believers in this event. But properly understood this does not indicate the defects but rather the essence of the event; for the point of the appearances is precisely the arising of faith in the Risen One. He did not show himself to everyone, he did not become an object of neutral observation. Nor can one say that the appearances presupposed faith in him. Rather, those to whom they occurred became believers. There is no account of anyone to whom the Risen One appeared who did *not* become a witness to the Resurrection. It is true that in every case knowledge of Jesus is presupposed, and that means that the question of faith has already been raised. This is also true of St. Paul. To this extent, therefore, knowing the Risen One meant knowing him *again*. There was not a communication or special and additional revelations, but solely the revelation of Jesus himself. He appeared as what he really was, namely, the witness of faith. But the witness of faith is recognised only when one accepts his witness in faith. The appearing of Jesus, and the coming to faith of him to whom the appearance is imparted, are therefore one and the same.

Yet this interpretation is not sufficient. For not everyone who comes to faith does so by way of such an occurrence. The appearances were limited to a narrow circle, and were not meant to be repeated. Paul himself clearly regarded the sequence of the appearances as closed with his experience. And a closer study of the list of appearances makes it clear that something unique and unrepeatable is happening, whether one considers the individuals or the groups to whom the appearances were vouchsafed. The unique and unrepeatable element indicates that the appearances had the character of a call. They completed the knowledge of Jesus which was necessary for the proclamation to be maintained.

But it would be quite wrong to explain this as meaning that those first witnesses had faith made easy for them by a miraculous event, whereas the rest had to be content with mere faith. This would lead to the grotesque conclusion that the first preachers of faith were not themselves dependent on faith, but were dispensed by seeing from the need for believing. Rather, we have to do here with a believing seeing. If we consider, say, the scene on the Damascus road, it would be meaningless to speak of a succession of events, Paul first seeing the Risen One, then being convinced of his reality, and only then deciding to believe. But rather, a single indivisible event takes place: Paul falls down in faith before the overpowering reality of the Crucified One.

The appearances of the Risen One are usually sharply distinguished from visions. But if we understand Paul's experience on the Damascus road as a vision, it is hard to see why the other appearances should have been fundamentally different. Paul himself does not recognise any such difference in the mode of the appearances. The decisive thing in all the encounters was that men were approached and overwhelmed and claimed by Jesus. Against all their natural attitudes and reactions, those who encountered him were awakened by him to faith, and called to follow him as the first witnesses of faith. The intensity of this basic encounter can be seen in the fact that it took the form of a seeing and hearing, though not for neutral eyes and ears. It would be wrong to construe these events by means of an ideal of a superior and direct mode of encounter with Jesus. For the first witnesses to the Risen One knew of no more appropriate mode of relation to Jesus than that of faith. It is not in the appearances as such, but in faith, that their witness is grounded. *Every* believer is summoned, as believer, to be a witness to the Risen One. For faith establishes a relation to Jesus himself. Christian faith is not faith in the apostles, and through them indirectly also faith in Jesus; but it is faith, by means of the *witness* of the apostles, in Jesus himself.

But now comes the most important task in interpretation—to go on from the historical analysis of the Easter tradition to explain what faith *in* Jesus really means. Why must this faith be faith in him as risen? What does resurrection from the dead mean? And to what extent is the believer dependent upon Jesus, so that his faith is not just kindled by Jesus, but clings to him and exists in community with him? In dealing with these questions we can expect that some light will also be cast on what is still obscure in the Easter event. All that I have to say in succeeding lectures about Christian faith will in fact have to deal with these questions. But meantime I make three suggestions which may help us to understand better.

First, what does the "basis of faith" mean? Certainly not a support which relieves us in part of the need for faith. Rather, the basis of faith is that which lets faith be faith, which keeps it being faith, on which faith, that is to say, ultimately relies. According to the biblical witness this is not the isolated and objectified fact of the Resurrection, but it is Jesus as the witness of faith in the pregnant sense of the author and finisher of faith.

Second, what does "faith in Jesus" mean? It means to let him, as the witness of faith, be the basis of faith, and thus to have to do with him and to enter upon his way: to participate in him and his way, and thus to participate in that which is promised to faith, namely, the omnipotence of God. To believe in the Crucified One, *this* Crucified One, in the witness of faith which he fulfilled in dying, means to believe in the omnipotence of God, it means to confess the power of the God who raises from the dead. To have faith in Jesus and to have faith in him as the Risen One are one and the same. But one cannot rejoice in the Resurrection of Jesus unless one recognises that the Cross of Jesus must now become the central content of the message of faith.

Third, what does "resurrection of the dead" mean? The best help for understanding this is to abandon any effort to form an image or ideas of it. That Jesus is risen from the dead does not mean that he returned to this earthly life as one who has death ahead of him once again. But it means that he, the dead one, has death (not just dying, but death) finally behind him, and is finally with God, and for this reason is present in this earthly life. What resurrection of the dead means can only be understood when we begin to apprehend what God means.

VI

The Truth of Faith

In our reflections upon the nature of Christian faith we must now take up the theme of " God." This in itself may be as surprising as the title, " The Truth of Faith," under which we take it up. If we consider what it is that strikes us as strange in this, then perhaps we have come to the theme in the right way. For to have to do with God certainly means in the first instance to have to do with something that is both surprising and strange.

It is true that the opposite view is widespread. If a poll were taken on the question, which part of Christian doctrine was the hardest to accept, or which part most resisted the understanding, and on which faith in practice was least nourished, then the answer would surely not be what is said about God—unless you were asking specifically about the trinitarian dogma. In this case the answer would be, " Of course I believe in God, but I can't make anything of this dogmatic extra, this teaching about the Trinity." And similarly, the general answer would be, "Of course I believe in God. But the rest of what I am asked to believe in the Christian message, especially about Christ, his vicarious suffering and dying, his resurrection and his coming again—all this is what I find strange and alienating, and cannot really get at. I am content with simple faith in the God whose commands are to be obeyed and whose mercy is to be trusted."

Now it would certainly be misguided to reply to this that it is all very well, but just too meagre; and that Christian faith means very much more than this mere faith in God, which Jews and Mohammedans, and even those who do not belong to any particular religion, possess. On the contrary, I should reply that indeed the only thing required is that we should acknowledge God. What gives rise to concern in those average reactions is that they take place almost as a matter of course. For this shows that they have no real apprehension of God. If there were this apprehension, then we should hear such responses as this: much in the traditional Christian expressions of belief is obscure to me, but this disturbs me only so far as it really has to do with God. For the question I really want a reply to is, what have those difficult utterances of belief to do with God? What do they contribute to my understanding of what the word " God " really means? For far from this being a self-evident presupposition and simple preparation for Christian faith, it is the supreme and extreme beyond which faith need not understand. What do I need except to learn what God really is? That is why the words that God is, which have become an empty phrase, contain within themselves nothing less than the entire Christian faith, and are not the easiest but the hardest of all to understand.

This is also the situation which has arisen in the course of our argument, when we direct our attention especially to the question of God. We have been speaking about God all the time, even though in a different way, when speaking of faith. For what is faith if it is not having to do with God? When we spoke of Jesus as the witness of faith, we meant that he bore witness to what it means to have to do with God, in death as well as life. And when we spoke of Jesus, the witness of faith, becoming the basis of faith, again we meant that in relation to Jesus we have again and again to do with God. This sounds as though the relation to Jesus consisted of mere imitation. Certainly the motif of imitation of Jesus has again and again played a great part in the history of Christian devotion. But if imitation means reproduction of certain outward attitudes, such as a life of unsettled pilgrimage and poverty, then this is not at all relevant. For faith cannot be imitated. Faith must be ventured on its own responsibility. Faith is the following of Jesus, if by following we do not mean the repetition of outward motifs, but solely the taking up of the innermost motif of the way of Jesus, namely, having to do with God, being committed to him. Jesus has become the basis of faith because, in face of the crucified witness of faith, having to do with God has received a radical meaning: the presence of the Crucified One makes it certain that faith remains pure faith. "He who believes in me," says the Christ of the Fourth Gospel, "believes not in me but in him who sent me" (John 12.44). To believe not in spite of, but because of, the cross of Jesus, that is, to believe in relation to his death, and in this way to have to do with God—this is to confess the resurrection of Jesus from the dead. That is, in face of this dead one we take seriously the words that "God is not a God of the dead, but of the living" (Mark 12.27). This does not mean that we regard the cross as a mistake in the divine administration which was happily put right straight away, or as a mere semblance which was quickly over. But it means that we so harmonise God and the cross of Jesus that this cross properly expresses, once for all, what it means to commit oneself to God; that this is why we believe as we look to this cross; that consequently the God who is believed is one who shows his true reality in death; and that to commit oneself to this God means to share in true life.

This was the point which led us to concentrate specially on the question of God. For in view of the fact that faith in Jesus regarded itself *eo ipso* as faith in the Risen One, we asked what "resurrection of the dead" really meant. We refused to approach this question by means of the ideas which human fancy is accustomed to fabricate about this event—an event which contradicts all our ideas. We noted that if "awakening from the dead" can be understood at all, then it must be only as God's action; so that it can only be understood if we begin to apprehend what we mean by God.

But if this is our concern, it does not mean that we give up interest in the history of faith and its essential historicity. We do not rise above, let us say, talk about Jesus Christ in order to elevate ourselves into the timeless fields of metaphysical speculation. Rather, we are concerned to think concretely what we mean by God, not beyond and apart from our real life, but in strict relation with it, so that God and ourselves are together in the one sentence. We shall have to speak of God in such a way that we ourselves are there too, with all that constitutes our real life, and are really affected. We shall not speak of God apart from space and time, but in respect of them, and of all that can affect and press upon us in space and time.

The sober way to express our real situation is to see our failure and fall, that is, to see guilt and death, which go together, for "the sting of death is sin" (I Cor. 15.56). This is the reality of our existence, that in the end we have no future. And if we now think about God concretely, in relation to this reality, then we have to hold firm to this contradiction, that on the one hand we hear in our existence the brutal and unambiguous words, " You have no future," and that on the other hand to say that *God is* can only mean that we do have a future. To think of God concretely therefore means to think of God in a contradiction. When we say "God" in this sense, we contradict the sharpest contradiction to God, namely, sin and death. Only in this contradiction can God be properly spoken of. This is the concrete point where alone God is spoken of. Any talk about God which is unrelated to this, is abstract speculation, and literally irresponsible, for it does not take place in the concrete responsibility of this reality of our existence.

Perhaps it is now possible to see why we speak of God as the truth of faith. Faith does not elude the question of truth. It does not put on blinkers. It does not bar itself from that which every reasonable man can see, and must see. But faith actually demands an honest and conscientious use of reason, and eyes which are open to reality. Faith is the sharpest foe of superstition and illusion. Nor does it take refuge in the idea of double truth. For to commit yourself to God means to commit yourself to truth being one. But though faith in this way pins everything to the question of truth, so that it stands and falls with it, yet it has to admit that the truth of everything it says depends on God.

To say that God is—or, in the careless and unthinking mode of speech that is common, that there is a God—is not an isolated truth to which other equally independent utterances of faith can be added. But rather, there is here a necessary and indissoluble connection. The truth of every utterance of faith depends on the one thing, that God is. And if they do not depend on God himself, this shows that they are not necessary utterances of faith, indeed, strictly speaking, are not utterances of faith at all.

Therefore the situation is not that one first manages to believe in God, and then so to speak builds up further articles of belief on this basis, so that faith in Jesus, say, has to be understood, if not as a rival, at least as an addition to belief in God. Rather, faith, wherever it speaks, and in all that it says and confesses—and faith is not dumb, but has something to say—is faith in God and the unfolding of this sole truth of faith. So in turning to the question of God we do not offer some special question for discussion, or some individual article of faith; but we are concerned with the truth of faith itself, with that on which the truth of all individual utterances of faith depends.

If God is the truth of faith, then the question of God also means the question of verification of the truth of faith. Does this not mean that we move in an ominous circle? For can the truth of faith be attested in any other way than by faith? Can God be recognised, can his being be acknowledged in any other way than in faith? Is not faith the sole proof of the existence of God, just because faith is the sole proof of the truth of faith? But in that case can faith be distinguished from illusion? If the truth of faith depends entirely on God, but the truth of God is nothing else but the truth of faith, then does each not just depend on the other, yet without giving it any support? What does one hold on to, when it is not this or that in the Christian faith but God himself who is called in question?

This is the situation we are in to-day, even though not many have realised it. We are exposed to atheism in such a way that it is not easy to take full account of the state of affairs. For we are bound to admit that atheism is a possibility belonging to our life and determining the reality of our existence. No words can scatter the mists that veil this strange reality from us more relentlessly than those of Nietzsche about " The Madman." One can never become accustomed to them, and even those who know them well need to ponder them again. I quote them now.

" Have you not heard of the madman who lit a lantern at noonday, ran to the market-place, and cried unceasingly, ' I am looking for God! I am looking for God!' Since it happened that there were many standing there who did not believe in God, he roused great laughter. Is he lost? said one. Or gone astray like a child? said another. Or has he hidden himself? Is he afraid of us? Has he gone on a voyage? Or emigrated? So they shouted and laughed. The madman leapt into their midst, and pierced them with his glance. 'Where has God gone?' he cried. ' I will tell you. *We have slain him* —you and I. We are all his murderers. But how did we do it? How could we drink up the sea? Who gave us the sponge to wipe out the whole horizon? What did we do, when we unchained this earth from its sun? Where is it moving to now?

77

And where are we moving to now? Away from all suns? Do we not stumble all the time? Backwards, sideways, forwards, in every direction? Is there an above and a below any more? Are we not wandering as through infinite nothingness? Does empty space not breathe upon us? Is it not colder now? Is not night coming, and ever more night? Must we not light lanterns at noon? Do we not hear the noise of the grave-diggers, as they bury God? Do we not smell God decaying? —Gods too decay! God is dead. God stays dead. And we have slain him. How shall we console ourselves, chief of all murderers. The holiest and most powerful that the world has ever possessed has ebbed its blood away beneath our knives— who will wipe this blood from our fingers? What water can make us clean? What propitiations and sacred rites will we have to invent? Is not the greatness of this deed too great for us? Must we not ourselves become gods, in order to seem worthy of them? There was never a greater deed, and because of it all who are born after us are part of a higher history than ever was before!'

" The madman fell silent, and looked at his hearers again. They too were silent, and looked at him with shocked eyes. At last he threw his lantern on the ground, so that it broke in pieces, and went out. ' I come too early,' he said, ' it is not yet my time. This monstrous event is still on the way—it has not yet penetrated men's ears. Lightning and thunder need time, the light of the stars need time, deeds need time, even after they have been done, in order to be seen and heard. This deed is still further from men than the remotest stars—and yet they have done it.' The story goes that the madman went into several churches on the same day, and sang his *requiem aeternam deo*. Led out and questioned, he replied just the one thing: ' What are the churches, if not the tombs and sepulchres of God?' " (*Fröhliche Wissenschaft* 125.)

The Truth of Faith

It is part of the historicity of faith that the way in which it is contested changes, and this does not happen in any casual fashion, but in an irreversible course. Moreover, faith itself is a participant in the changing attacks to which it is exposed, and is itself a cause of them. Serious opposition by pagan polytheism is long past. For long periods of church history faith may be seen as attacked almost entirely from within, by false security, for instance, or by self-complacency, forgetfulness, and indifference. At all times there has existed this practical but unconfessed and veiled atheism. It is true that in classical antiquity, and through the middle ages, in a tenuous line, there was something like theoretical atheism. But it is in modern times that something quite new and unprecedented has arisen, namely, atheism as a mass phenomenon. As it was once one of the great matters of course that there are gods, or that there is only one God, so to-day—although in not inconsiderable circles the old matters of course continue to be effective —it has become a new matter of course in very wide circles that there is no God, that he is mere fancy, just a word, and that one neither needs to reckon with him nor to expect anything from him, that he is dead, and that there is no future in believing in him. This is the same in the east and the west, whatever the superficial differences.

It is a cardinal error to identify this phenomenon, which is indeed not far from any of us, with that superficial and trivial atheism which consists of easy-going self-forgetfulness, and is allied to a lack of bounds and of stability, to presumption and despair. Nietzsche perceived very clearly the difference between this vulgar atheism and its lonely counterpart, which in its passionate search for God looked into the shuddering depths of an atheistic fate. And in this atheism, which is breaking in like an inexorable fate, another distinction must be made, between its more or less militant assertion, surrender to it without a fight, and the self-critical entry of Christian faith into the changed situation of faith. What we simply must not do is hide our heads in the sand and avoid the questions which this raises for faith.

For the source of modern atheism is closely connected with Christian faith. Only where God is so radically proclaimed and believed can he be so radically denied. But it would be an improper simplification to reduce the connection to this antithesis alone. For a radical Christian faith contains the seed which de-divinises the world and makes it truly the world. In the form of modern secularisation of all spheres of life this has spread like a spring tide over the whole world, and propagates, more rapidly and effectively than the Christian mission spreads faith, a mere consequence of Christian faith.

Furthermore, Christianity has also a guilty connection with the pre-history of modern atheism. We think, for instance, of the split in the church in the west, which led in the end to the need for keeping a broad realm of life free of confessional strife, where tolerance and neutral co-existence were practised. Step by step all spheres except religion itself were thus treated—politics, law, morality, science were emancipated from the hegemony of the Christian claim to truth, a claim which had become denominational and thus no longer generally binding, and were subsumed under their own principles and laws. Or we think of the understandable yet quite devastating way in which the churches, both Protestant and Roman Catholic—with differences, indeed, but without difference in their guilt—in the name of Christian faith opposed insights which were undoubtedly true, and which in the end were triumphant in any case; suppressed the right of free inquiry; misled men's consciences; established the unavoidable stumbling-block of faith in quite the wrong place, and thus brought into confusion not only the understanding of faith but also the love of truth and truthfulness. Our judgment in these matters must be sharp, for we are still suffering from the consequences; moreover, in some church circles the guilt incurred by the church has either been long forgotten or never recognised. It is no wonder that the idea is widespread that the Christian faith is a reactionary power both in political and in general intellectual matters, whereas atheism stands for science and progress.

Or finally, we think of what presses most immediately upon us, that the proclamation of Christianity is clearly unable to destroy the caricature of the Christian faith which it itself has brought into being, and which is now held against it in propaganda or in the genuine embarrassment of incomprehension. Assurances are of no avail that this or that is the real meaning of Christianity, and that Christian faith is quite misunderstood when this or that is attributed to it. The only possible course is to give an uncompromising account of the nature of Christian faith in the context of our total awareness of truth and understanding of reality. In opposition to the view that the problem can be dealt with by apologetic patchwork at this or that point, or by a defiant and complacent disregard of genuine questions, theologians to-day are gradually becoming aware that we face a task of translation and interpretation which permits nothing in theology to be regarded as a matter of course and without need of being thought through. For the burning task of interpretation includes the question what " God " really means. In the eighteenth century, in the optimism of the Enlightenment, it was thought that the idea of God, with the help of compelling proofs of reason, could be made into an unshakable basis for understanding. Then in the nineteenth century it was thought that there was at least a universal religious a priori which could be a starting-point. To-day we face the question how, without the evidence of proofs of God's existence, and without the presupposition of a religious need for God, we may speak of God, and speak, moreover, in a way that is both understandable and relevant.

The first thing to be said in this connection is that to speak of God has the character of truth which is found in *faith*, and therefore not the character of an objectifying statement about some fact which can be verified outside faith. For God is not an objectifiable piece of reality. So far as objectifying thought is concerned, as it has come to prevail in scientific method, though in different forms in the natural and the humane sciences, God can *eo ipso* not appear. It is a banal matter of course that God cannot be spoken of in terms of the natural sciences, and that in terms of the humane sciences he can only be described and analysed as a moment in human self-consciousness. God can only be spoken of appropriately in personal commitment. For since to speak about God concerns and includes the one who undertakes to do it, its truth is of such a kind that the speaker must commit himself, in his own reality, for the reality of God; he must engage his own existence for the existence of God. Any speaking about God which does not make it clear that it comes from faith and leads to faith, threatens to obscure the fact that speaking about God concerns the truth.

The second thing to be considered here is that what the word "God" means can in the first instance only be expressed as a question, namely, as a pointer to the radical questionableness which touches every man. We have to do with the experience, proper to everyone, of a questionableness which embraces the world and myself. In the last resort this cannot be answered in any piecemeal way, but only with one's own person, which owes an answer. This radical question which a man encounters can be more closely defined as the experience of passivity. The decisive happenings of existence, birth and death, indicate the passivity which underlies all human activity. Whatever one's judgment about the question of God, it is clear that man is at least not his own creator, but has been thrown into existence without being given any choice of time or place or circumstances. Whatever one's attitude to death, it is clear that man must die, so that even if he takes his own life he is only anticipating the fate that awaits him. And in his existence between birth and death man is likewise in many ways—as one who is approached, summoned, commanded, questioned—delivered over to passivity. In the last analysis he is "passive" as one who is questioned, and that means also challenged to give an answer: he is asked about whence he came and whither he goes, and both questions are summoned up in the question about where he is. Adam, where art thou? For the present we say no more than that the word "God" is this radical question about where man is, the question which concerns him unconditionally. We can only say more than this when we have pondered the meaning of this last suggestion, that God meets us as the Word.

VII

The Communication of Faith

We spoke of God. But what we had to say was accompanied by a counter-theme, which came back again and again, and almost overwhelmed the first, namely, the theme of death. I am not thinking only of the discovery by the "madman" that God is dead. But at the very beginning of our theme there was the contrapuntal note that it was the death of Jesus which provided the occasion to speak of God. For the meaning of resurrection from the dead can only be grasped when we begin to understand what God means. On the other hand, it is only in opposition to death and sin, its sting, that we may speak concretely of God. This dissonance of death and God sounded out again at the end of the last lecture, when we asked how in this modern world we may speak of God in a way that is both understandable and relevant. And our provisional answer to what the word "God" means was to look at the radical questionableness which unconditionally touches every man as man, in the question about where he is: where art thou? But does speaking about God to-day really reach this point where man is unconditionally approached in his questionable nature? Nietzsche with his "God is dead" made a definitive judgment which is gaining more and more ground. He was saying that to speak, as the Christian does, of the living God, who makes the dead alive and called what is not into being, has become incredible. Thus to speak of God at all carries no conviction. And indeed, if God is no longer heard as the contradiction of death, one no longer has a right to speak of the living God. In that case Nietzsche's words, "God is dead," would be eminently meaningful. In both cases, one must add, there is a like ignorance of God, whether one says "God is dead," or speaks abstractly of God, without the contradiction of death.

A fatal error is possible here: the conjunction of God and death in our theme might lead us to suppose that to meet death means to meet God, and to meet God means to meet death. As though death were the one clear point where God were to be encountered. This would end in a terrible confusion of death and God. In seeing the close connection between two mutually exclusive elements, we undoubtedly made the question about the truth of faith as sharp as possible. Nor do we wish to withdraw anything. Yet it would be fundamentally wrong to identify this sharp setting of the question, this ultimate depth and critical boundary, with the thing itself. We spoke of the truth of faith as the crisis of faith. But this does not dispense us from now having to speak of the truth of faith as the communication of faith. There is a danger in the Christian's speaking about God that *it* should settle down on that extreme critical boundary and thereby deprive it of its character as the critical boundary: this would mean losing the truth of faith. For who has any experience of death? When the Christian speaks about God he likes to bring in death, this gives his talk its seriousness and its significance, and it usually includes the demand to clothe yourself, outwardly and inwardly, in black, as though talk about God were like going to a funeral. To take part in a funeral is as little a real encounter with death as to talk about God in funeral mood is a real encounter with God. The talk about God which is really understandable and relevant is that which sees life itself as the place of encounter with him, and not death or some artificially induced funeral mood. God enters into real relation with death for us only when he is understood as the one who encounters us in the midst of life.

The Nature of Faith

For to speak of God as the one who encounters us is clearly to speak of the reality of God. For how should his reality be experienced except in an encounter? At the end of the last lecture I said, God meets us as the Word. What does this mean? Can it mean that the meeting is a second thing alongside speaking of him? Or is not speaking of him the only way in which he meets us? But in that case would not the God who meets us as the Word be nothing but a mere word, a thought? And how could this be called a meeting?

The title of this lecture, "The Communication of Faith," is intended to make clear the meaning of God meeting us as the Word. But it seems to be ambiguous. For "communication" can be understood to mean the communication of something, as in a newspaper or the like. But "communication" can also mean providing a means for sharing, in the sense of the Epistle to the Hebrews 13.16, in the words "to do good and to communicate, forget not." In the first sense "communication" is simply speech, in the second sense it is a doing, and perhaps at its best a doing without any words. In the first sense it is made available for knowing, in the second sense for experiencing. Or the two senses may be distinguished in this way, that in the first I have experience of a *thing*, even if the communication should have to do with a man; whereas in the second I experience a benefit, I experience love, that is, something happens to me. In the first case I take part simply as an observer, in the second I really share in an encounter.

These two different ways of communication could be further depicted and analysed. Then it would soon appear that the distinction is not the last word, and that it is no accident that the two modes can be described by the same word. For even a wordless deed of communicating mercy says something to the recipient, far beyond the gift that may have been given, and in this respect the deed also has the character of a word. Similarly, the communication of knowledge by means of words also has the character of an event; it establishes a definite mode of sharing in what is communicated, and can also become a gift which touches the man himself, even changing his situation. For instance, a communication which I receive can communicate joy to me, in such a way that my joy is not just a casual reaction to the content of the communication, but is a sharing or participation in the joy of the one who brought me the communication. The real communication, in this case, would not be the news which gave me joy, but the joy itself. One can say that in such a case the real content and the effect of the communication are one and the same.

It is by such considerations that the dimension of the word as an event can be disclosed to us. We are accustomed to think of words chiefly as the bearers of a definite sense, of a content of ideas. We too easily overlook the fact that the real power and significance of words lie in their effecting something, aiming at something, even when it is just a matter of "information," and quite certainly in the mode in which more than information is communicated, when one communicates himself to another, and so by means of words there takes place a "having together with the other." Meeting in the deepest sense is not something that takes place apart and separated from words, but it happens in the event of speech. The phrase "communication of faith" therefore does not mean mere communication about faith, instruction about the intellectual contents of faith, but it is intended to express the communication of faith as an event in the event of speech. The content of the word and the fulfilling of the word, its reaching its goal, are identical. A word of this kind does what it says, it fulfils what it promises. When faith and God are put together, we may put it thus: we are not concerned just with a piece of information about God, but with participation in him, that is, with an event in which God himself is communicated. If what I have already briefly said is right, then such a communication would be a true meeting with God, and it would not be in the least preposterous, but perfectly appropriate, that this meeting with God should take place in the word as an event.

Of course, it is not any and every word about God that is a communication of faith, that is, that can communicate the faith which is a participation in God himself. To use the language of the biblical tradition, it is the Word of God alone which can do this. But what does this mean, "the Word of God"? How is this concept of the Word of God to be delimited, in order to bring out clearly the extraordinary and unique element in it? Two contrasting concepts demand attention. First, the Word of God apparently demands that it be understood in opposition to the word of man. Second, as God's own Word it is clearly opposed to a word about God, in which God himself does not speak, but is only the object of speech. Both delimitations are useful, and indeed in one sense indispensable. But at the same time they are open to misuse which causes great confusion in the meaning of God's Word. We must therefore examine these distinctions more closely, and we begin with that between the Word of God and the Word about God.

It betrays an inadequate understanding of the Word of God to argue, on the basis of this distinction, that there are many, perhaps too many, words about God, all the groping, unclear, false or at least unauthoritative talk about God. For who could be authorised to make adequate and absolutely valid assertions about God? Can there be anyone whose talk about God does not stick in his gullet, as soon as he really tests himself, and asks, "Do I really understand what I am saying? Can I really be answerable for it, and responsible for what I say? Or is it just chatter, ignorance of the depths of the mystery, misuse of the name of God, an insult to his divine majesty?" Now though everyone has reason enough to test himself in this way, it is thought that there is one exception to the general questionableness of talk about God. It is said that besides the invalid and inadequate talk there is also the valid, authentic, and adequate Word about God, which is not thought up or thought out but revealed. God's own Word is what is to be found in the Bible. The characteristic of the Word of God would then be that it is an authentic, revealed Word about God. The essential difference is apparently brought out at this point.

But it is nevertheless not so, if the Word of God is merely regarded as the sum of many words about God, reliable communications about God, providing so to speak complete enlightenment about God, because miraculously inspired, but still remaining within the sphere of that same view of words, namely, that they merely communicate knowledge. If the concept of the Word of God is to have meaning, it must lead to a more adequate and more radical understanding of what the Word means.

If we stick to the popular understanding of *word* as communication of knowledge, then we merely encourage the views which make the concept of the Word of God seem absurd. Then it looks as though we are dealing here not with a literal way of talking, but with the way of images and symbols. As it would contradict the biblical view of God to take expressions like "God's hand" or "God's mouth" literally, and to imagine God as a physical being with hands and mouth, so it seems to be with regard to the expression " Word of God." This cannot mean the Word that God himself speaks, but just the Word that corresponds to God. On this line of argument the " Word of God " would then be simply another way of describing authoritative speech about God.

Now we must certainly admit that if we understand by "Word" nothing but an articulated word in a particular language, and if we speak of God as a heavenly super-being, then it is true that we can regard "Word of God " only as a symbolic mode of expression. Otherwise the question would arise once more, which was once seriously discussed, what language God speaks, whether Hebrew, or (as pious Russians thought) Russian. But we are not to imagine God as a super-being who is with himself, and is therefore a piece of the reality of the world. Nor may we limit the real meaning of *Word* to a grammatical structure or something which we hear.

If we follow these indications—which are in line with the biblical intention and with the doctrinal tradition of Christianity —then the "Word of God" is not just a symbolic mode of speech, which could perhaps be better replaced by the vaguer concept of "revelation." But the concept, the "Word of God," properly understood, provides the most striking expression for what happens to man from the side of God, that is to say, for the way in which God deals with man. For with God word and deed are one: his speaking is the way of his acting. We must be prepared, in matters of the language of faith, to win free of the traditionalism which clings to formulas without understanding them and without making the responsible effort to realise them. If we refuse to do this, the really important thing, faith itself, is abandoned in favour of certain *ideas* of faith which we think cannot be given up. Now the concept of the Word of God holds the key position in the relation of faith and language. If we found it necessary to regard talking of the Word of God as an unreal, and strictly speaking inappropriate mode of speech, then the whole Christian way of speaking of faith would be called in question. For the nature of Christian faith depends upon God himself speaking in the Word.

But is there not an insuperable difficulty in the fact that the concept, the Word of God, *eo ipso* requires to be understood as opposed to the "word of man?" The antithesis we have already discussed seems to be repeated here. For a word about God has clearly the character of a human word. But is this not also true of God's Word, so far as it has to do with a comprehensible word which can be addressed as God's Word? Is it not then an un-avoidable consequence that we can only have God's Word in the shadowy, unreal and veiled form of a human word? " Human word " is in fact a tautology. The only words we know are human words in human language. Non-human words, if we may speculate in this way, would not only be incomprehensible, but they could not even be experienced as words. Therefore, when we speak of a Word of God which we encounter concretely, which we can hear and understand, we always mean God's Word in the form of human words. But in that case what is the meaning of the distinction between God's Word and human words? And how may their relation to one another be conceived? Must we adopt the very questionable view that a particular sphere of clearly human words—let us say, the Bible—is only apparently human words, but is in fact an exception, having come into existence under supra-mundane conditions, and requiring corre-sponding methods of interpretation, which do not apply to other human words? Or must we search for some kind of compromise solution, that God's Word and human words are related as kernel and husk, as eternally valid content and temporally conditioned form?

These are all illusory solutions, which can only lead us astray. For to ask how God's Word can enter or be transformed into human words is itself an illusory problem. For this kind of question, which sounds so eminently reasonable, and exalted above mythological thinking, labours under the strange delusion that God first of all speaks in some language of his own which is unknown and incomprehensible to us, which then requires to be translated into human language—or some particular human language—which like all translation will be successful only to a limited extent. Such a view would be appropriate if it were a matter of man having to solve the riddle of God's hiddenness, to decipher the hieroglyphics and symbols behind which he lay hidden, and make them comprehensible. Of an undertaking of this sort we could only say that it falls far short of its goal.

But if we take seriously the fact that God turns to man, claims him, addresses him, then it is meaningless to ask how he can do this in a way that man can understand. For this turning to man is God's humanity. His Word which is directed to man is as such a human word. There is no trace of a difference. And if we try as it were to excuse God and explain that in his condescension he adapts himself to man's limited comprehension, then we misconceive God's Word, imagining that it does not really express what he has to say. The only way to maintain the expression " God's Word " is to recognise that it gives clear and full expression to what is essential. For if God's Word should mean anything else than this concerning his love, then should we not rather regard the whole thing as human fantasy and desire, and simply say, " It is not true"; instead of limiting God's Word with all kinds of reservations, such as " It is not exactly clear what God's real meaning is, and of course we can only speak of his love in inverted commas, for since there is a qualitative difference between God and man everything in respect of God is quite different from what it sounds in human words." The answer to God's Word can only be, " Yes, it is true, this is exactly how it is." Here there is no room for spinning out interpretations and multiplying problems. But where God's Word comes, it comes as what is simply essential, it is unambiguous and it creates clarity.

Of course we must speak of the difference as well as the identity between God's Word and human words. This does not meet the difficulty how any divine meaning can be expressed in human language. Rather, it concerns the difference which consists in whether man or God is speaking. This difference can only be grasped as an opposition. The way in which God and man are differentiated in respect of the Word cannot be more simply formulated than in the words of the Old Testament. " God is not man, that he should lie " (Numbers 23.19). " All men are liars " (Psalm 116.11). And Paul takes up the refrain: " It will appear that God is faithful, but every man is a liar " (Romans 3.4). Man's words in themselves are lies. But God cannot lie. What he promises, he surely keeps.

This is connected with the fact that man has a different aim from God. Man's will is not conformed to the will of God. In the depths of his heart man wishes that God were not, that is, that God were not God and did not behave as God. God, on the other hand, keeps in his heart " thoughts of salvation and not of perdition, to grant you a future and a hope " (Jeremiah 29.11). He does not have " pleasure in the death of the godless, but rather that he should turn from wandering and live " (Ezekiel 18.23). Luther repeated this basic motif of the Bible when he said that God is "a glowing oven full of love." In line with this, he explained the real opposition between God's Word and man's words as follows:

" As often as God's Word is preached, it makes the conscience joyful in face of God, it enlarges it and gives it certainty. For it is a Word of grace, a good and beneficial Word. But as often as man's words are proclaimed, they make the conscience sad, narrow and fearful in itself. For they are words of the law, of wrath and of sin, showing what we have not done, and all that we ought to do." (WA 2; 453.)

If we may reduce this matter to a short formula, God's Word is the " Word of faith," whereas man's words are "mere moral words, without faith" (WA 2; 462). That is, man's words can at best only demand, but they cannot communicate what it is the mark of God's Word to communicate, namely, faith.

I sum up this intricate matter by indicating the main outline of the argument.

First, the meaning of the Word of God can only be grasped

on the basis of the gospel. It vitiates our understanding of the concept if we try to define it formally, as though anything one liked could be the content of the Word of God. It is God's Word because it is God who comes to speech in it, and this speech is the revelation of his humanity in his turning to man. Therefore it is not many things, nor remote and transcendental mysteries, but quite simply one thing, the one necessary thing, which is necessary for salvation, the one simple clear thing, for it is light, just as the essence of the Word is true light.

Second, the Word of God is the communication of faith. For the Word of God and faith are inextricably joined together. Since God desires faith, his revelation takes place as a Word. The true gifts of God are not what one can see and grasp. The gift of God comes only in virtue of the Word which is bound up with it, to which faith holds fast. The Word expects that he to whom it is spoken allows it to be spoken to him, and depends upon it. Because God promises man salvation, and a future, his Word opens up the future, it encourages trust in God, it is a Word of promise which communicates faith. If this is God's saving will, that man should believe, man is directed to the Word which communicates faith.

Third, for the sake of his Word and in his Word God enters history, he becomes historical. For it is the Word which in the last analysis makes history. Where God enters history, the arch stretches from what is said to what the Word has as its goal. There life is lived in memory and expectation, between past and future. There God is present as " he who is and was and is to come " (Revelation 1. 4).

Lastly, if we ask, where then is God's Word, the Christian message points in the first instance to him of whom the Gospel according to St. John says, " The Word became flesh " (1.14). That is, it points to the witness and basis of faith. So it will also point, further, to the Bible as the record of faith. It will also point to the whole event of this Word as it is attested in the history of faith. It will do all this in order to answer the question, " Where is God's Word? ", with the one answer: " Here, where the proclamation of God's Word takes place, here and now, in the concrete communication of faith." So this proclamation of the Word of God will also speak of the whole of reality which concerns man. It will also, in order that it may be a comprehensible and relevant proclamation of the gospel, speak of the law by means of which man is approached by God, before ever the gospel is preached. For it is only through this connection of law and gospel that God's Word is comprehensible and relevant.

Since we are trying to understand the meaning of the Word of God, we must now turn our thoughts to the Holy Spirit.

VIII

The Courage of Faith

In what we have already said about faith, and especially about the communication of faith, all questions and reservations and objections were supposed to be settled. But now our theme of the courage of faith proposes that nevertheless there is still outstanding a question, inarticulate perhaps, but rising up in us. It may be formulated thus. One last decisive thing is required in respect of faith. Should we say, one last decisive step? Or a last decisive leap? At any rate, the question is, how do we reach faith? It is true that we have already spoken of the communication of faith, that is, the Word of God. But even here, was there not something still left open? Is there not a gulf between the communication of faith and its fulfilment in truth and reality?

It could be asked whether we can get any further by talking about faith, and whether all that is left is the decision to believe, the leap into faith. And that is clearly a matter of courage. It needs courage to dive into the water from the high-diving platform. It needs courage to trust the parachute, which only open as it falls, and to let oneself fall into the yawning depths from a great height. Likewise, and yet incomparably more, it needs courage to depend on nothing in the world at all, but let oneself, so to speak, fall into God. Luther, with his extraordinary modernity of speech, once described the happening of faith in these terms:

What does a man reach who hopes in God, save his own nothingness? But whither shall a man vanish, who vanishes into nothingness, except to where he came from? He came from God and from his own nothingness. So he who returns to nothingness returns to God. For he who falls outside himself and all creatures, whom God's hand embraces, cannot fall out of God's hand. For he holds the world in his hands, says Isaiah. Fall then through the whole world—whither do you fall? Into the hand and the lap of God. (wa 5; 168.)

Certainly it needs courage to believe, that is, to have to do with God. To trust God means to leave oneself and the world. Christ said, " I leave the world and go to the Father " (John 16.28). And of his disciples it is written that " they left everything and followed him " (Luke 5.11). For Jesus summoned them to faith with the call not only to renounce all they had, but also all they were. " He who will follow me, let him deny himself" (Mark 8.34). And yet doubts cannot but arise when faith is described as letting oneself fall, as a leap into nothingness in order to fall into God. It was the voice of the tempter which said, " If you are the son of God, cast yourself down. For it is written, He will give his angels charge concerning you, and they will bear you in their hands, lest you dash your foot against a stone. To which Jesus replied, It is also written, Thou shalt not tempt the Lord thy God " (Matthew 4.6f.). Further explanation is needed—though certainly not in order to meet faint-heartedness half-way, but in order that we may not confuse the courage of temerity or of despair with the courage of faith, the spirit of evil with the Holy Spirit. For the "courage of faith" means the Holy Spirit.

When I said at the end of the last lecture that we must now speak of the Holy Spirit, the context was different from the present line of thought. What I said there about the Word of

God ended with the question, "Where is the Word of God?" And I pointed to the Christian proclamation, which in proclaiming the gospel must also bring in the law, through which, before any preaching of the gospel, men are approached by God. For the gospel is the joyful message of the fulfilling of the law, of Christ as the end of the law; so that the communication of faith is also freedom from the law. We must therefore know what the law means, if we are to be clear about what the gospel is. In order to understand the Word of God, we have to learn to distinguish between the law and the gospel. For the gospel can only be preached with intelligibility and power when its relation to the law is understood. And I ended by saying that in order to understand the Word of God we must turn our thoughts to the Holy Spirit.

So now we have two juxtaposed suggestions why we need to turn to the Holy Spirit. First, the Spirit gives understanding to faith, and second, the Spirit gives courage to faith. What joins the two is that the Spirit opens the way for faith, by overcoming the resistance to it. We know that faith is hindered both by a lack of understanding and by a lack of daring, or, more strictly, by a lack of willing. For where courage is lacking, the will is lacking. But let no one think that this is an easy matter. Certainly, I can change the objects of my willing. But to change my will itself, to give it an entirely different direction, means no less than changing myself. And strictly speaking this is impossible for man. For he cannot lift himself by his own boot-strings. He cannot himself, by his own willing, alter his will. For this, as the Christian message says, he needs the Holy Spirit. We can therefore ask which is the stronger hindrance to faith, lack of understanding or lack of courage; and whether the Holy Spirit is needed in greater measure for illumination, in order that we may understand, or for encouragement, in order that we may be able to will. But there cannot be any rivalry between the two points

98

of view, as though the Holy Spirit could only be defined in one way or the other. Rather, it is the coincidence of the two which must be asserted. For as not understanding can be the cause of not willing, so also not willing can be the cause of not understanding. In fact, in the last analysis both come from the same root, and only thus can they be properly grasped. And the work of the Holy Spirit can likewise only be properly grasped when the changing of our blindness into understanding and of our lack of will into courage are seen not as two but as one and the same.

From another aspect, however, there does seem to be a serious rivalry between two points of view. Does having the Holy Spirit not mean much more than to be dependent upon faith alone? Are we not more directly in touch with God when we share in his Spirit, than when we are merely dependent on his Word? Is it not a fateful abridgement of what Christianity really should be, if the Holy Spirit is given, so to speak, a mere auxiliary position to the paramount relation of the Word and faith? This is what the Reformation appears to have done, and what we are now imitating, if we allow to the Holy Spirit only the power to give understanding to the Word and courage to faith. Does this not reduce the Holy Spirit to the level of what is normal and accustomed? And whether this takes place within the church, or within bourgeois society, does it not imply a domestication of the Holy Spirit which is clearly a sin against the Spirit? For the Holy Spirit is the extraordinary. Throughout the history of the church we may see movements of protest against Christianity being reduced to a matter of church or society, being turned into a normality when in fact it shatters every norm. For the Spirit blows where it will (cf. John 3.8). " Do not quench the Spirit " (I Thessalonians 5.19). Where the Spirit is given freedom, must not extraordinary things happen—words of prophetic authority, even ecstatic speaking with tongues, healing of the sick, outstanding sanctity of life? Such movements of protest, which appeal to the Holy Spirit, have been called sectarian and fanatical. But are they not closer to early Christianity than the kind of Christianity which is domesticated within the church and society?

In opposition to this kind of thinking it must be emphatically said that every appeal to the Holy Spirit which thinks that it is superior to mere faith and the Word is at any rate not the Spirit of Jesus Christ. The Christian understands the Holy Spirit as the Spirit of Jesus Christ. On the other hand, all talk about faith which clings to the Word must be quite clear that the Holy Spirit has a part to play in this. Otherwise, it does mean that faith is dissolved in mere piousness and the Word of God becomes a religious law. For the Holy Spirit, far from being a rival of the Word of God and of faith, is the happening, the realising, the very presence of what the Word of God and faith really mean. To speak of the Holy Spirit means to emphasise the actuality of the communication of faith. It means that the truth of faith, of which we speak, really happens and is present. The Bible compares the Holy Spirit to wind and fire. For the Spirit is not a static possession, which now and then becomes active. But he is activity and motion, and therefore sets in motion. Where the Spirit is, there is storm and fire. One cannot be seized by the Spirit and remain in one's old ways, inactive and immobile. To be kindled by the Holy Spirit means to glow and burn, so that you are a source of movement and warmth, affecting others. Without metaphor, which might mislead, this is not a destructive force, like the senseless fury of natural powers unleashed, but it brings healing and life, true healing and true life, in accordance with God's ordering, whose Spirit is life itself, and thus creates life, *Spiritus Creator*.

If we wish to interpret the Holy Spirit in terms of what we have to say of Christian faith as the courage to believe, we must justify the use of the word "courage," which otherwise might seem an arbitrary use. It is very difficult to express with the word "spirit" what the Holy Spirit really is. Sometimes "spirit" just means a "ghost," sometimes it means something that man is equipped with by nature, in more or less degree. Sometimes it means the so-called objective spirit of nations, religions and civilisations, that is, a supra-individual historical phenomenon. Or it may even mean something like the intellect, when Ludwig Klages, for instance, speaks of the "spirit" as the antagonist of the soul. It may also mean the inner élan of enthusiasm which surges over all the inhibitions of the theoretical intellect. There is still another variation in the modern usage of "spiritual" which tends to have nothing to do either with spirit or with enthusiasm.

If we set aside for the present the Christian influence, we may simplify the matter by saying that we use the one word "spirit" for two Greek words, *nous* and *pneuma*. The image appropriate to *nous* is the unchanging clarity of the light in which things stand for the gaze of the observer. The image for *pneuma* is the blowing of the wind, which catches one up in its movement. The one is connected with timeless truth, the other with living power in temporal existence. This distinction is not found in the Old Testament. The Hebrew word which is used of man's spirit, but especially of God's Spirit, is very near to the Greek *pneuma*, except that it has a personal quality in contrast to the more natural sense of the Greek. But there can be no doubt that what was understood and experienced in Christianity in relation to Old Testament thought as "Holy Spirit" was expressed in Greek by *pneuma*, and never by *nous*. And characteristically, the point at which the Holy Spirit comes upon man is not the upper or "spiritual" level in man, in the sense of the Greek *nous*, nor indeed is it those obscure levels of the half-conscious and the unconscious, of the instincts and passions, where the Greeks regarded the *pneuma*, even the religious *pneuma*, to be located. But the Holy Spirit strikes the "heart," which means the inmost centre of personal life. So the Holy Spirit, which is a new and renewing Spirit, creates a new heart, turns the "heart of stone" into a "heart of flesh." That is, the Spirit awakes the heart and conscience of man, that is, man himself, to real life from God and before God. For wherever the word "spiritual" or "Spirit" is used in the New Testament sense, the criterion for its proper use is this double relation, "from God," and (what I should call the relation of encounter) "before God."

We do not wish to try and find a substitute for the word "Spirit." But we must take note of the nuances of meaning which are present in it, coming from other concepts. In English the word "courage" is customarily used in a rather narrow sense; but its derivation indicates its relation to the heart, which it stirs and whose life it determines. We speak also of "spirited," and it is in this direction that the word "courage" is here used: this means much more than a matter of mood or fancy: it indicates the inmost heart of man, especially when his life is threatened. A "spirited" man, or a man "of good spirit," is at one with himself, so that his whole being is directed by his "heart." This is what "courage," or being "of good courage," means: that a man is not divided, or in doubt; he does not stand in his own way, he is not consumed by self-contradiction, nor does he deceive himself. He affirms himself, and does not give up. It is different with the man whose heart fails him, who capitulates before difficulties, who is discouraged by them and is therefore his own betrayer, and gives up. It is in this sense that courage is needed for human living, not courage at this or that point but courage for life itself. The man who is completely discouraged cannot go on living. The man who has access to inexhaustible springs of courage is able not only to live but also to die without losing heart. For when they are properly understood the courage to live and the courage to die are one.

We cannot discuss here, with the precision that is really required, the relation between this general account of courage, and the New Testament understanding of the Holy Spirit. But would anyone wish to controvert the assertion that Jesus Christ became the source of true courage, the courage which comes from God? The New Testament sayings about the Holy Spirit open up a large area of discussion, which we cannot properly examine here. But we must recall some of the main lines, since they are little known among the theologically uninstructed.

First there is the fact that in early Christianity, as it understood itself, the experience of the Holy Spirit was the very signature of its existence. The intensive use of these two words is an outward expression of this. It is noteworthy that there is no record for the combination of these words, holy and spirit, in secular Greek. The usage is a biblical creation, occurring seldom in the Old Testament, but more frequently in Judaism. If a Christian were asked what was really new in Christianity, he would not have spoken of a new teaching, but he would have pointed to the new reality of the Holy Spirit. The Old Testament prophets spoke of the Spirit as the gift of the last days. And in late Jewish apocalyptic this connection between the gift of the Spirit and eschatology was intensified. In early Christianity these two factors are very closely connected—that they regarded themselves as an eschatological community and that they thought of their existence as determined by the Spirit. It is from this standpoint that we have to understand St. Paul's reference to the new covenant, in relation to the old, as the Spirit which makes alive in contrast to the letter which kills (II Corinthians 3.6). In place of the law there is now the real happening of that which the law demanded in vain. In his appeal to the experience of the Galatians he offered them this alternative:

" Did you receive the Spirit by works of the law, or by hearing with faith ? " (Galatians 3.2.)

Second, the experience of the Spirit and faith in Christ are closely connected. This is true of the whole New Testament. Faith in the Risen One and the outpouring of the Spirit cannot be separated, even though the later tradition formed two centres of gravity, namely, Easter and Whitsun. In the farewell discourses in the Fourth Gospel we find this close connection between the Christ to be exalted by dying, and the sending of the Spirit. The primitive confession of Jesus is the very language of the Holy Spirit. " No one can say ' Jesus is Lord ' except by the Holy Spirit " (I Corinthians 12.2). So the Holy Spirit and his work are wholly bound up with Jesus. The Johannine Christ says: " But the Counselor, the Holy Spirit, whom my Father will send in my name, he will teach you all things, and bring to your remembrance all that I have said to you. . . . He will glorify me, for he will take what is mine and declare it to you " (John 14.26; 16.14).

Third, we must distinguish between the confession that every Christian, as incorporated in Christ in faith by baptism, shares in the Holy Spirit, and the experiential background to this, that in Christianity the Holy Spirit is at work with very various gifts and effects of the Spirit. It seems to have been St. Paul who was the first to oppose, by means of this clear distinction, the danger of enthusiasm running wild. By setting the gifts of the Spirit under the discipline of the Holy Spirit as given to the whole community and all its members, and thus regarding these gifts from the point of view of service, St. Paul drew the definite boundary between Christian faith and fanaticism.

Fourth, the Holy Spirit is neither a natural part of man (his better self), nor does he become man's possession. But only he has the Spirit who lets himself be possessed by the Spirit, in the sense that he is led and impelled by the Spirit, who dwells in him as God in his holy temple, from sheer grace. The consequence of this gift of the Holy Spirit is that man becomes a battlefield between Spirit and flesh. Man exists only in participating in powers which are not himself. Spirit and flesh on the biblical view are not two parts of man, but they are two powers which continually claim the entire man. Even the most splendid things in man, including his religiousness, without the Holy Spirit are simply "flesh." But on the other hand, even the most insignificant and unpretentious things in human life are destined to be the instrument of the Spirit. For the gift of the Holy Spirit is no more than the pledge of what the Spirit as Sanctifier is able to effect in man, to the point of the resurrection from the dead.

Finally, we must try to answer the question concerning the connection between what we have said about the Holy Spirit, and what we have said about faith. There are three points to note.

First, the relation between the Holy Spirit and faith is not to be defined in terms of two opposed powers, regarded as making separate claims for credit. In man they are basically one and the same. What we affirm concerning the Holy Spirit—that he sets free, makes alive, makes men into sons of God, that he is the source of sanctification, and so on, together with all the fruits of the Spirit which he effects in man—all this can likewise be affirmed of faith. Even linguistically the concept of faith and the concept of the Spirit in the New Testament stand in a remarkable correspondence to one another. They both express what Christianity really is. Nor would it be right to denote their connection by simple addition, nor, further, to say that the Holy Spirit is the work of God and faith is the work of man. For properly speaking faith too is the work of God. All the same, the emphases differ: man is always the subject of faith, whereas, if we may so put it, God is always the subject of the Spirit. That is to say, faith and the Holy Spirit are the two aspects of the one event, namely, of that which has become new in the relation of God and man in virtue of Jesus. We said earlier that faith is man's participation in God; we may now say that the Spirit is God's confirmation of this participation. And when we said that the Spirit gives courage to believe, this does not mean that the Spirit is additional to faith, or simply kindles it, but that the Spirit is the permanent character of faith as a gift, which has its life entirely from the divine confirmation. " I believe; help my unbelief " (Mark 9.24). So when faith prays for the Holy Spirit it prays for faith to be given again and again. For faith confesses, in Luther's words in the " Explanation of the third article of faith in the *Little Catechism*," " I believe that I cannot believe in Jesus Christ or come to him of my own reason and power, but the Holy Spirit has summoned me through the gospel, has enlightened me with his gifts, and has sanctified and maintained me in right faith."

Second, this relation of the Holy Spirit and faith determines the relation of the Spirit and the Word. The Spirit is not something different and higher which has been promised alongside the Word. But the Word of God, that is, the gospel, is the communication of faith, and it is really this in so far as it is the communication of the Holy Spirit. For God has given his Spirit in the Word, that through the Word he might give the Spirit. God's Spirit is not a special substance, but is God's self-expression in his Word. Therefore, his Spirit is not additional to or beyond history, but is God himself present in the midst of history in virtue of his Word.

Lastly, the early Christian Creed expressed the unity of the Holy Spirit and God by expounding the one faith in the one God as faith in God the Father and in Jesus Christ and in the Holy Spirit. This was then given precise form by developing theological reflection in the trinitarian dogma. In speaking of the truth of faith, of the communication of faith, and of the courage of faith, this trinitarian way of speaking of the God of our faith has pressed itself upon us. Let this hint be enough. For Christian faith is not directed to the trinitarian dogma, but to the God who in three-fold form, as the truth, the mediator and the giver of faith, as Father, Son and Holy Spirit, summons us to faith and maintains us in faith.

IX

The I of Faith

When we speak of faith we must speak of man. This does not compete with the other assertion, that when we speak of faith we must speak of God. For it is of the nature of faith that because we speak of man we must speak of God, and vice versa, because we speak of God we must speak of man. A theology which is oriented towards faith cannot make God its theme without making men its theme; nor make man its theme without making God its theme. For "God and man" are not two themes, but one. To separate God and man misunderstands both. God and man are only known in relation to one another. There can only be knowledge of God if thereby man reaches knowledge of himself. And man can only have self-knowledge if thereby God is known. True knowledge of God is not of God in himself. For a neutral, objective knowledge of God, which sets him at a distance, is a contradiction in itself. True knowledge of God is of God who is for us and with us. And similarly, true knowledge of man is not of man in himself, in abstract isolation. In the last analysis man is abstract, isolated from the reality which concerns him, when he is not seen in his relation to God.

In all our discussion hitherto we have taken this structure of all theological affirmations into account. For they are assertions of faith, and as such are determined by the nature of faith. Even when our first concern was God, his Word and the Holy Spirit, we were also talking of man. How can it be otherwise, when all our considerations about the nature of faith have been oriented towards Jesus Christ, of whom faith confesses that he is "true man and true God?" Nevertheless, in the exposition of affirmations of faith it is both fitting and necessary to shift the emphasis; so it is now necessary to look at man in particular.

It is man whom faith affects. But we must ask what this means. We could say that faith contains knowledge and insight which affect man directly or indirectly. This is man's place in the affirmations of faith. And these affirmations are only understood as such when a man knows that he is affected by them. But how does this affecting take place? It would be misleading to say that man must simply take over these affirmations of faith, appropriate the truths and views and ideas contained in them. For that would make it seem that we had to add the contents of faith to our stock of truths and views and ideas—or even replace in part the old stock by these new ones—and thus to propose a change in the stock of what one *possesses*, in the present case, one's knowledge and insight and convictions. But faith primarily affects man himself, not what he possesses, however serious the consequences of faith for what he possesses or does not possess, including his money. Faith concerns, it touches man primarily in what he *is*. For "believing" is not a thing, but an event; it is primarily as a verb and not as a noun that its reality is seen. If we speak of the reality of faith we must add the person who believes, because he is affected by the communication of faith. The I of faith must come into the picture. And being affected in this way is not adequately expressed, or at least not without a possibility of mis-understanding, by the phrase, I have faith; nor by the expression, I am a believer; but simply by the words, I believe. It is not the learning of concepts of faith, nor is it an inner structure of a believing piety, but it is the grasping of the communication of faith which is the way in which faith happens. Faith is only real when it affects the man himself, when it is an event which takes place in him and through him, whose subject is this man. To speak of faith as an event means to speak of it as personal. Not *it* believes, but *I* believe.

This is why the responsibility attached to all speaking of faith becomes especially acute, when we turn to man as being the I of faith. The investigation of this I of faith is comparable to the critical function of experiment in the natural sciences. For this raises the question of the experiential and verifiable reality of all that has so far been said and has still to be said, whether and in what way it is more than theory and ideology, and concerns man in the reality of his existence. We must use this criterion ruthlessly and without pretence; we must not omit any phenomenon of man as he actually is in his basic nature, nor cling to some special or artificial reality of man concocted in the interests of religion. The mark of a real concern for faith is truthfulness in the account that is given of it when it is confronted with the possible and actual experience of every man. So much talk about faith is mere pious jargon, without any real self-criticism, that this temple needs to be cleared and cleansed of its decadence.

It must be admitted that to bring man and faith together in this way, to speak of " I believe," that is, to speak in truth and certainty of man as the " I of faith," is opposed on practically every side, even if from very differing motives. It must be emphasised that we are speaking simply of man, not of a man equipped with some special talent, but of man as man, so that everyone is summoned to believe, and no one is excluded. Faith is therefore something which concerns every man, to which he is summoned simply because he is a man, and for the sake of his life as a man. Further, we are not speaking of the I of any faith, but of *the* faith which is our theme, and by which everything is to be confirmed as true. On the one hand, resistance to this talk of man as being the I of faith arises from the side of unbelief, in all its variations, ranging from outspoken hostility to faith to that pretended faith which is not recognised as such by itself or others. All along this line man appears to refute faith, whether he lives in open contradiction of faith or in hypocritical contradiction of his human existence. In all these variations man is disclosed not as the I of faith but as the I of unbelief. And on the other hand, from the side of faith, must we not admit that man can only be understood as the I of unbelief? And if the miracle of faith does take place, is it not a pure gift, not a work of man but exclusively a work of God in man? And must we not identify the Holy Spirit with this I of faith, and not man at all?

Let us begin with this second objection, which argues from the nature of faith that man himself cannot be the I of faith. Now we must in fact hold fast to the truth which is expressed here, and on the basis of which everything else about the Christian message of faith is to be understood—namely, that faith is not a work of man, but the work of God in man, the gift of the Holy Spirit, the simple opposite of all achievements and all merit, and nothing that man can boast about. For someone to boast about his faith would be quite senseless, it would indeed abolish faith. For faith is the end of all one's boasting. Otherwise, how could faith alone justify man before God and sanctify him, if it were not God who were at work, who alone can sanctify man and make him right? Or how could faith mean participating in the omnipotence of God, if it were not the end of human power and possibilities, so that God alone is at work? How should faith, and nothing but faith, be the attitude due to God, unless it makes room for God's nature, his omnipotent mercy, his being as creator, and renounces every claim of man's own worth? So St. Paul, looking at the Corinthian community, provides sober illustrations from his experience:

" For consider your call, brethren; not many of you were wise according to worldly standards, not many were powerful, not many were of noble birth; but God chose what is foolish in the world to shame the wise, God chose what is weak in the world to shame the strong, God chose what is low and despised in the world, even things that are not, to bring to nothing things that are, so that no human being might boast in the presence of God. He is the source of your life in Christ Jesus, whom God made our wisdom, our righteousness and sanctification and redemption; therefore, as it is written, ' Let him who boasts, boast of the Lord.' "

I Corinthians 1.26ff.

On the other hand, it is neither arbitrary nor unrealistic to speak of faith in this personal way, which makes man responsible for faith, as, for instance, in the question and answer in adult baptism: " Do you believe? I do." Even at that point where St. Paul, looking at the believer's life, simply abolishes the life of the human I as subject, he says, characteristically, " It is no longer I who live, but Christ who lives in me " (Galatians 2.20); but he does not say, and could not say, " It is not I who believe, but Christ who believes in me." For the believing that takes place in my own I *is* the change in mastery and guidance which concerns my whole existence, my life as a person. We must therefore say that both are alike essential to faith: both its divine character as a gift and its being always my faith, being really faith when it is a responsible action and commitment of my person, in a faith which is my own and nobody else's. To confess one's faith is part of faith, and to commit oneself personally is the meaning of confession.

The extreme form of witness and commitment is martyrdom, and this is simply the manifestation of the essence of faith when it is fully realised. That our faith is our own, irreplaceably, is connected with our dying, which is equally our own and irreplaceable. Instead of martyrdom, which we may consider to be a rather remote possibility, let us think of the normal situation in which our faith is irreplaceably our own, namely, the situation in which every believer is tempted, and in which death is still to come, with its power of being the extreme temptation of his faith. When Luther returned from the Wartburg, and summoned the Wittenberg community back from fanaticism to the way of faith, he spoke with unexampled clarity and emphasis:

> We are all alike summoned to death. No one will die for another, but each in his own person will fight with death for himself. We could indeed cry into one another's ears. But each must be sent by himself in the time of death. I shall not be with you, nor you with me. In this everyone must know for himself what matters, what a Christian must do, and be armed. (WA 10.3; 1f.)

It would be wrong merely to see a contradiction here, and to say, although faith is a work of God, yet it is I who believe; or to say, although man is the I of faith, yet faith is the gift of the Holy Spirit. For the point is that the two go together, and are not mutually exclusive. For faith and freedom are inseparable. On the usual view of the freedom of faith this connection of faith and freedom is obscured. For in the religio-political sense the freedom of faith just means the freedom to believe what you like, even not to believe at all. It also means a freedom on which faith depends, which must be granted to faith; but it does not mean a freedom which faith itself discloses and confirms. Certainly, we have no wish to undermine a view of the freedom of faith to which we owe the freedom in which we live, and which we are fully conscious of only when we see other conditions in which this freedom is stifled. (Though the view does exist, for reasons of parity, so to speak, and from the standpoint of him before whom all are sinners, that all intra-human differences, including those between East and West, should be abolished. But it only makes for confusion to see no difference between absolute and relative propositions.) Therefore, it is not because we despise this so-called freedom to believe, but just because we wish to preserve it, that we criticise the usual view.

It is certainly beyond dispute that faith and compulsion do not go together. But it would be wrong to say that faith must not be coerced. For faith *cannot* be coerced. It can be hindered by coercion—and that is the peril where freedom to believe is lacking; but it can also be hindered by the attempt to compel faith. For it is not enough to explain why faith cannot be coerced by saying that coercion only determines the externals, and thus in certain situations may breed hypocrisy, while the inward life of faith cannot be touched by coercion. Unfortunately this is not true. We have frightening examples of this to-day. In fact, the spread of human power is much more perturbing to-day in the development of the most subtle methods of spiritual oppression and depersonalisation than in the developments of physical and technical power. It is unfortunately true that man's inmost life can be violated by coercion, so that to that extent we must say that there can be something like coercion of faith. That this is nevertheless self-contradictory, and properly speaking impossible, lies in the nature of faith. For a faith which is enforced, and driven in by suggestion, would in fact prevent faith, which, at any rate in its Christian form, *is* freedom. Faith makes the believer free. This freedom which is disclosed by faith lies behind every freedom vouchsafed to faith. For in the sphere in which freedom can be vouchsafed to faith, faith has already assumed freedom in its own way, or, more precisely, made use of the freedom which is given to it in virtue of its being faith.

What, then, is this freedom which is of the nature of faith? It consists in man's being free of care. This is true in the concrete sense of not caring about food and drink and clothing and the morrow. But in a deeper sense this comes from the freedom from guilt and death. And this freedom in turn is man's freedom from himself. For the care which makes a man a slave is man's care about himself. Guilt and death have this enslaving power because with them man's care about himself, raised to its intensest pitch, leaves only two ways open—ways which are only different at first, for they aim at the same goal—either to suppress the care by self-boasting, or to rush ahead of it into despair. It is not that man sees himself as inescapably questioned about where he is and what his life means, which leads him astray; but that he walks in a path which can only cover over or intensify his care, namely, by clinging to himself in increasing self-seeking. And it makes no difference whether this is shamelessly open, or concealed behind its opposite of self-loathing.

In contrast to this, faith means to be free of self-care, and thus free in the most radical sense. From this there follows a fourfold clarification.

First, we now have light on the question we started from, namely, how faith as the work of God, the gift of the Holy Spirit, is related to the personal responsibility of " I believe." This is not a contradiction, for the gift of faith aims at giving man true freedom, and man's true freedom can only be a given freedom. Man's true freedom consists in his receiving himself from elsewhere, that he does not owe it to himself that he is, that he is not his own creator and therefore cannot free himself from himself. It is a psychological misunderstanding to regard this as a contradiction of man's freedom and personality—a misunderstanding due to bad psychology. For it is the mystery of human personal being that it is summoned from elsewhere, that it exists in response and as response, and that man is therefore wholly himself when he is not caught up in himself, but has the real ground of his life outside himself.

Second, faith concerns a man in a much more radical way than is supposed by bad psychology. It is not located in some partial or secondary level of his being, in such human capacities as the ability of knowing or the will or the feelings. If this were so, there would be no reason why faith should not be a human achievement alongside other activities and attitudes. In that case, the character of faith as a gift could only be maintained by having recourse to ideas, bordering on magic, of an infusion of spiritual power coming from beyond man. But faith is located in the personal being of man, deciding and determining him in the depths of his being. We could put it thus: faith has to do with the question where man's real place is. If the question, "Adam, where art thou?" is the most radical question which can be addressed to man, this question receives in faith the answer that man's place is not in himself but in Christ. In New Testament language this "being in Christ" is faith, and the New Testament interprets faith as the decision about where man is, where he lives and is at home. This decision of faith, therefore, is the being of man which precedes all that he does, and is the determining source of what he does or does not do.

Third, faith is not something added to man's being. It is not, so to speak, a luxury reserved for those who are talented or demanding in matters of religion, which only they can or need afford. For the aim of faith is to bring man to his true humanity, to let him be the creature and son of God, in the ever renewed pressure of the unity of creation and redemption. The believer, therefore, is not a superman, but true man, because he has come to the truth, and that is why faith decides about what concerns every man, and concerns him unconditionally, i.e. concerns his salvation. The real task of Christian proclamation to-day is to learn to speak of faith in such a way that it ceases to be regarded as a specialised religious matter, and is clearly seen in its demand on man as man and in its decisive liberating power over his whole being.

Finally, we may begin to have an inkling of what sin really is, namely, that what by moral standards is usually called sin is no more than a consequence of man's real sin, which is unbelief, sin against the first commandment.

So the question about the I of faith points now to the further question how the I of unbelief can become the I of faith. What is this turning from unbelief to faith, which is not just a change that happens to man, but a change of man himself, a change of such a radical kind that it is described in terms of dying and being born again, and moreover must be paradoxically formulated as involving not the pious man but the sinner as the I of faith?

X

The Reality of Faith

The question of the reality of faith was implicit in what we said about the " I " of faith. It was bound to be, for faith is not taken seriously if it is regarded as something separate from the rest of reality, whether as a vague pious mood, or as the sum of certain religious ideas, or as a highly developed theological system. In such ways faith is under suspicion of being mere froth, an ideological illusion which is opposed to reality. This is the impression of Christianity which underlies the sharp criticism of which Feuerbach and Nietzsche are the chief exponents. The modern form of unbelief finds its justification by questioning the reality of faith. Anyone concerned with faith must take account of this criticism, if he is to check the danger of schizophrenia which is such a widespread threat to Christianity to-day. For faith and the understanding of reality are in danger of breaking apart, so that the Christian thinks and lives in two entirely different systems of thought, in the everyday world of work and play on the one hand, and on the other hand in the Sunday world of religious ideas. Nor does it help, on the contrary it only increases confusion, to lay claim, in a stubborn and emotional way, to a concept of reality for the so-called world of faith which is just as massive as the concept used elsewhere. For this merely encourages a meaningless juxtaposition which falsifies both the nature of faith and the understanding of reality as a whole. But it is equally fateful, in the understandable fear of falling under the tyranny of a false view of reality, to avoid altogether the question of the reality of faith, and to use dialectical subtleties to settle every question about experience and the relation to real life. A great deal of theological effort is perversely determined to exclude disturbing questions which seem naïve and crude by professional theological standards, but which in fact in an elementary way are at the very heart of the matter. Certainly, the truly elementary questions are the most uncomfortable and the hardest. To be open in the right way to the question of the reality of faith is not a matter of slick theological solutions; but it presents a task which lasts all one's life. For this is one of the problems which cannot be simply solved and settled, but must be gone over again and again; for its demands upon us never cease, so that we are pupils who are always far behind with our task.

We must therefore link this question to that of the I of faith. For, as we have already said, to speak of faith is to speak of man. For it is man whom faith encounters in such a way that he is the I of faith. And in considering this I of faith, we have to ask about reality, and experience, and the confirmation of all that has to be said about faith. In Christianity everything is concentrated in faith, so that to discuss the nature of Christianity means to discuss the nature of faith. This again means that in Christianity the question of what is gropingly called "religious reality" is directed in an unusual way towards the real existence of man. A whole host of misunderstandings can arise at this point. To mention just one for the moment, it is wrong to suppose that this question about the I of faith necessarily gives faith an ominously individualistic bent, and that to concentrate upon faith means that we have decided in favour of an individualistic view. For though faith certainly concerns man in his irreplaceable self-being, it does so in the entirety of his real existence, for which an individualistic interpretation would be completely inadequate.

Nevertheless, the I of faith is not the same thing as the reality of faith. For however much the discussion of the reality of faith points us to man as the I of faith, and however much the reality of faith can only be expressed by reference to man's real existence, yet the real existence of man and the reality of faith are not identical. What we have said about the I of faith was merely preparatory to a proper discussion of the reality of faith as a separate theme. For it is not man who gives faith its reality. Faith is not something that can be sketched in at the right place within the framework of the given reality of man's being. It does not receive its lasting reality from man and the framework of his possibilities. If that were indeed so, then Pelagius would be right when he said that man's salvation came from the exercise of his free will, and Ludwig Feuerbach would also be right, because more logical, when he said that the secret of theology was anthropology. Our consideration of the I of faith brought us to the fundamental assertion that faith is not man's work, but God's work upon man. This, as we said, does not result in the paradoxical abolition of the fact that man is the I of faith; but rather it explains it. For man's freedom, which is disclosed by faith, indeed is faith itself, can only exist as a gift. This leads us to conclude that we cannot explain faith by any concept of reality which we care to apply, but that we must bring our view of reality itself into the closest connection with faith and what we have to say about its reality.

Here we approach the very heart of the matter, where we encounter the hardest and most elementary problems of Christian faith. Once again I propose some theses, briefly and without much argument.

First, it may be a source of surprise, and even of bewilderment, that with this theme " The Reality of Faith " I intend to present simply the so-called doctrine of justification. Yet this is the point on which simply everything depends: the reality of faith *is* the justification of man. " For we hold that a man is justified by faith apart from works of law " (Romans 3.28). If this is true, then from these words of St. Paul we may directly derive the nature of faith, what it does and brings about, what happens only in faith and nowhere else, what its exclusive reality is, and what is so indivisibly joined to it that the two are completely one—namely, justification. Faith is real only when it is justifying faith. Faith which does not justify would be a mere fiction, an imitation, the product of fancy. This determines faith, and is the criterion of its reality, that it justifies. Faith in common parlance can be understood as not justifying. But on a proper theological understanding the word faith must always be used to mean justifying faith. It is of the essence of faith that faith alone justifies.

But this needs further explanation. Three points of view must be clarified if we are to understand this matter of justification properly. What view of reality is here presupposed? What, in this context, is the meaning of those difficult expressions, "righteousness" and "justification"? And what is the real relation of the so-called doctrine of justification to justifying faith itself?

Of the first question we must say that it is not quite correct to speak of a view of reality as presupposed. For this gives rise to the idea that there is a view of reality which is quite independent of the doctrine of justification. The connections which we are touching upon here are very complicated, both historically and in their nature, and they cannot be properly unfolded without thorough philosophical, theological and historical treatment. I confine myself to the general remark that there stream out from Christian faith effects which penetrate the general world of thought as well. It would be shortsighted to suppose that the consequences of faith are limited to the circle in which faith is affirmed and lived—to put it crudely, to the circle of influence of the church. When Christian faith arose, the historical world as a whole was changed. Irrespective of whether one is a believer or not, man since Christ is in a fundamentally different situation from man before Christ. This is susceptible of a profound interpretation in relation to the story of man's salvation. But we leave this aside for the present, and content ourselves with the observation that for every man who thinks historically there is a recognisable sense in which Christian faith has brought with it highly significant and irreversible consequences, which are apparent both in the history of the world and the history of the spirit. This can be seen in the realm of politics, of culture and art, as well as in morals, in the general awareness of truth, in scientific thinking and of course in philosophy as well. There is good reason for the illustration of such connections which is so frequently adduced to-day, namely, the role which Christian faith has played in the rise of historical thinking and in the de-divinisation of the world.

When we say that Christian faith has made the world different, we do not intend to make a moral value-judgment, as though Christianity had made mankind better. The possible objections to this kind of assertion have been so thrashed out that it is unnecessary to go into them here. Another tendency, to hold Christian faith responsible for a catastrophic development of world history, is so superficial that it need not be considered. We are thinking rather of a change in the relation to the world, of a transformation in basic thought-forms and the view of reality, which cannot be approached simply with the aid of standards of value. However, one could say that these changes have intensified the possibilities of both extremes, to good and to evil, and that therefore the opposition of human possibilities has been sharpened.

These remarks are merely intended to indicate the wider background to the point that Christian faith has had effects upon the general view of reality which are to a certain extent separable from their connection with Christian faith. But it is for me a significant fact that this indication of general historical consequences of

Christian faith should arise in a discussion of the doctrine of justification. For this prevents any misunderstanding of faith as something purely inward and private. Certainly, those consequences of faith are not the reality of faith itself. But justification as the reality of faith is to be seen as having public significance, and concerning the world as a whole.

I must now try to describe briefly the view of reality which is implicit in the belief in justification. We are far too ready to talk of a man in the same way as we talk of a thing or an object when we think about it, describe it or judge it. So we think of him as something complete and entire within himself, equipped with certain qualities and capacities. If we want to know who this or that man is, or what man in general is, or correspondingly, who God is, we take him as an entity for himself, and determine his qualities. Thus in traditional philosophical ethics a doctrine of virtues is constructed, and in the doctrine of God his attributes are described. Even if, in a specific circle of discourse, it is significant to speak in this way of man or God as something that is in itself, and so to describe them on the basis of their attributes, we must nevertheless maintain that this is an extremely abstract approach. One might go further, and describe the objectifying view of things, especially in the sciences, as a deliberately abstract approach, in which the concrete living relation to things is left out. The chemist has a structurally different relation to the bread that he eats than to the bread that he analyses.

But we will stick to the discussion of man. It is surely clear that an approach which objectifies and isolates man threatens to destroy what is peculiarly human, or at any rate leaves it out of sight. The relations in which man finds himself are a part of him: his environment, other men, himself, and—in it all—God. They are not additional to his life, but they constitute it; and this may be seen in the way a man regards his worth in relation to his self-understanding and to how he is understood or judged by others.

It is illusory to suppose that everything that happens to man, or that human life itself, is to be understood in terms of facts. Rather, in human life there is the closest connection between being and understanding, existence and encounter, what one has and what one is worth, between what already is and what is still to come, past and future. For it is of the essence of human—and that means of historical—reality that nothing is finished, but there is always something to come, something to expect. Even the reality of what is historically past has its future, so that one can even say that it is futurity which constitutes the reality of what is historically past. Only that which has a future is real. That which has no future is nothing. Salvation in the strict, ultimate, that is, eschatological sense, comes to him to whom in his nothingness the future is opened.

We leave this brief discussion of the first point, and turn to the second. How are we to understand the difficult terminology of the so-called doctrine of justification? Only on the basis of Old Testament usage, in which the Pauline usage is rooted. In the Old Testament the righteousness of God does not mean an attribute of God, in the way that in Greek philosophy justice means the virtue of giving everyone his due. But in the Old Testament God's righteousness means an action of God, which always sets things right, creates salvation, through God's acting in accordance with his covenant, that is, in accordance with the communal relation which he has established. When St. Paul says that the righteousness of God is revealed in the gospel, he means that his act of salvation is revealed, only with this difference from the old covenant, that this righteousness is revealed in the dying and rising again of Jesus. For in Jesus the only righteous One, who is loyal to the covenant, has taken upon himself God's judgment upon the sinful life of all men without exception, is obedient even to death on the cross, and is therefore raised again and exalted by God. And now everyone who affirms this in faith, and acknowledges that God is right, is adjudged righteous, not because of works of the law, but solely of faith.

It cannot be denied that the language which St. Paul uses here is strange to us. And a much more extensive exegetical treatment would be required in order to make clear the inner connections of St. Paul's doctrine of justification. The view has therefore been maintained—and it undoubtedly is the feeling of most Christians to-day—that this Pauline doctrine is something very remote, which cannot adequately express the nature of faith for modern man. This teaching is regarded as something peculiar to St. Paul, which it would be an imposition to take over for to-day, especially as basic Christian teaching. It was thought that support was lent to this view by the fact that in St. Paul's own teaching the doctrine of justification was clearly confined to his controversy with the Jews. In other words, this could be regarded as a way of expressing the significance of Jesus Christ which was entirely conditioned by the particular circumstances of time and place. When St. Paul spoke to the Gentile Christians of Corinth he used quite different language.

This argument is right only to a limited degree. For there can be no doubt that in his doctrine of justification St. Paul expresses his most profound and radical views of the gospel. Moreover, we should have to ask whether other interpretations which St. Paul provides are really more accessible to modern man, for instance, the views which he bases on the Hellenistic mystery religions. For in my opinion the decisive Pauline view of the gospel would be lacking, if we made use of certain elements in his teaching in order to interpret him solely in terms of mystical piety. On the contrary, I believe that it is only with the help of his doctrine of justification that the depths of his message can be disclosed to modern man, and indeed that it is here that we find the clearest recognition, in the whole of the New Testament, of what faith really is. If we had to yield at this point, it would be questionable whether we could preserve Christian faith in its purity. And only by considering what pure Christian faith is, can we express what the reality of faith is, in such a way that it is comprehensible and convincing.

It is true that such assertions can carry conviction only if they can be proved, that is, if I can so expound them that what is difficult becomes basically simple, what is obscure becomes quite clear, and what is historical becomes a present word in which the reality of our own life is addressed, exposed, set in motion, and transformed. Yet who would maintain that he can do all that is required in this respect? We can only try, within the limits of our own capacity, to spell out the most elementary truths.

To do this we must first turn to the third point, namely, the question of the relation of the doctrine of justification to justifying faith itself. It must be said with all possible emphasis that justifying faith is not faith in the doctrine of justification. To put it as pointedly as possible, you may not know the first thing about the doctrine of justification, and yet you may partake of justifying faith. And on the other hand a knowledge of the theology of the doctrine does not in the least guarantee participation in the faith which justifies. This simple insight meets with opposition which often seems quite insuperable, on account of the almost ineradicable view of faith as a series of acts corresponding to a series of objects of faith, in which the significance of the faith is controlled by the particular object in view. No doubt this is a caricature, but I fear that it suits certain prevalent ideas: if I believe in God the Father, this means that I enter into a special relation with him. If I believe in the substitutionary suffering and death of Jesus, then I share in his merit. If I believe in his Resurrection, then I receive the powers of the Resurrection reality. If I believe in the Holy Spirit, then I am exposed to his presence. And so one could go on to the corresponding assertion, that if I believe in the message of justification from faith alone, then I share in this justification. One would think that the foolishness of this view were clear enough. For faith is one and indivisible. And any explication of it does no more than outline its nature. So faith is always justifying faith. As faith in the creator faith is nothing else but justifying faith. Then we might ask, why should an explicit doctrine of justification be necessary? In order that faith may be protected and confirmed, kept pure and real. The function of this doctrine is therefore primarily critical. To this extent it is a doctrine which in the first place concerns theologians, who are responsible for the truth and purity of the communication of faith. But since it is of the nature of faith that the believer should come of age, within the limits of his talents and capacities, so within these limits he must try to be clear about his faith, and able to judge about its purity and reality. That is why the doctrine of justification from faith alone lies at the heart of what I have to say.

What kind of reality has this faith which consists of justification?

Its reality is obviously of the nature of an event, which effects a total transformation, and yet never becomes a possession, but remains an event—the justification of the sinner which lasts as long as the sinner lives.

This brings us to the end of our preliminary observations about justification. We must now discuss its relation, as the reality of faith, to man as the I of faith.

XI

The Power of Faith

The titles of the lectures are intended to mark our progress along the way, as well as to indicate new directions. They may also be regarded as questions. Certainly they are questions of faith, that is, they are asked in faith, they are set by faith to us, so to speak as consequences, as what we have let ourselves in for, when we ask about faith. But however much it is the nature and the inner logic of faith which dictate the questions and drive us on from one question to the next, still these questions are at the same time set to faith by unbelief, much as the prosecuting counsel moves inexorably from one question to the next, in order to get at the true state of affairs. And when the subject under examination is faith, it must be cross-examined by man, and that means in the first instance by the non-believer, till the ultimate and decisive questions are reached, namely, those of the reality and the power of faith.

There is a danger that these questions are wrongly set, through being controlled by a misleading view of reality and power. But it is our basic thesis, without which our whole effort would be meaningless, that there does in fact exist a remarkable correspondence between faith and unbelief, an analogous structure in their nature. That is why the questions of faith and of unbelief, despite the sharpest opposition, run along the same lines. For their subject is the same, namely, "man between God and the world." And if faith is under cross-examination, so too is unbelief. This means that man himself is being cross-examined by the questions which in one way or the other belong to him. So we must not take offence at the ambiguity of the question about the power of faith. Certainly we have first to decide the sense in which it is to be understood, whether that of faith or of unbelief. But in either case it is a decision which concerns the question of power. For the conflict between faith and unbelief is at heart the question of their power. Faith or unbelief is in the last analysis a question of power.

We shall not pause to discuss the relation between this subject and the last one, the reality of faith. There is much which could be said, especially as the individual subjects are intended not to displace but to supplement one another. Nor have we concluded the discussion of the reality of faith. But perhaps by the present shift of emphasis we can indirectly do justice to it as well.

But there is another possibility of offence in turning to this new subject, which must be discussed. It seems very ominous to discuss faith in terms of power. Does this not mean that we are subscribing to a set of categories and to a certain tendency which are determined by unbelief, and are thus prejudiced against faith? Should we not by now have reached the view that the will to power, or even just being hypnotised by the question of power, is the basic evil? And should there not be a change of thought at this point, so that we keep our distance from this question, deny it, refuse to sully our hands with it, and turn to infinitely more important questions? In the struggle for power is it not the case that faith is always at a disadvantage, whereas unbelief is in its element, since it can give itself without inhibitions to this matter? Is it not simply impossible to believe when one is under this spell? Is this not the simple either-or that must be uttered when the decision of faith is to be heard and understood to-day: either to persist in the spell of superstitious belief in power, or in faith to be freed from this deadly plague? Would this not show a truly pure heart, and real faith—to be wholly immune to matters of power? Would it not therefore be much more appropriate to speak, not of the power of faith, but honourably and simply of its weakness and defencelessness? And such objections from the side of experience seem to find support from the standpoint from which above all faith desires to be regarded, that of truth, of righteousness and of justification. Does it not do irreparable damage to truth, if we bring in the question of power? And does the purity of the question of justification not depend on its being clearly separated from matters of power?

There is so much that is true and persuasive in these objections that we are tempted to reverse our whole line of argument, and establish a quite undialectical antithesis of faith and power. It is a remarkable fact, however, that this desire can readily assume another form, and turn into the view that it would be best not to speak of faith at all. For as the history of faith shows, it has again and again, in many different ways, been mixed up with the story of power. It seems to be in the nature of faith to be prone to get involved with power, and indeed under certain circumstances to push the question of power to extremes. Have not the worst power conflicts always been those of faith? Would it therefore not be better to abandon the subject of faith and turn to that of love? And if not in the sense of hostile antithesis, at least by combining the two, in the sense that faith without love is not real faith, that only love can give faith proper form and life, and that the reality of faith is therefore love?

Yet must it not be apparent that in such a shift in the argument the dominating theme again becomes the question of effects, of success, of fruits and usefulness—all of which means the question of power once more? In such a situation we should again be anxious about faith, though for other reasons, and this time lest in its subordination to love it should cease to be pure faith. And does such a concentration on the theme of love not inevitably raise the question of power in another sense, namely, when we ask where in this world of brute realities and lovelessness we shall draw the power for love? Does this not demand immense faith in the power of love? So we are brought back to the theme from which we started. For there is no doubt that, from the standpoint of power, faith and love go together. And we must not be put off by the formulation of this connection in a way which needs perhaps to be freed from sentimental overtones, but which, when properly understood, says all that has to be said: " I pray to the power of love which is revealed in Jesus."

To ask, then, about the reality of faith means to ask about its power. This cannot be excluded, if we are dealing with man in his historical reality. We have already said that only that which has a future is real. And certainly, what is historically real has to do with power in the sense that in existence the question is what is valid, what continues and endures, what emerges in the end: to put it crudely and pragmatically, the question in existence is what is effective and successful. What we understand by success, effectiveness and power, by what is ultimately enduring, has also to be decided; and in deciding what we mean by power the question of power in historical existence is also decided. To ask what the success of faith means takes us therefore into the depths of existence. Life is decided by faith. In faith, the question of power is decided in a twofold way: there is an ultimate decision about the meaning of power and about the struggle for power.

How else would it be possible to pledge your life as a witness of faith, except in the certainty that you are not despising life or lightly throwing it away, but laying hold in all seriousness of true life? This border situation throws light on the situation of faith at all times, that it carries with it the certainty that you are taking your stand on what is ultimately valid and reliable. You are trusting him who keeps his promise, who has the last word. You are relying on what will be fulfilled, on what nothing can hinder, against which no resistance is possible, whose power is superior to everything else. So to trust this power, to rely upon it and give yourself to it, is in the truest sense rewarding. I do not mean the reward of merit, of an inauthentic and calculating aim; but I mean rewarding in the sense of a certainty, which is identical with faith itself, that faith is not a way into nothingness, where all is lost and at an end, where everything is seen to be vain, but a way of salvation, where everything is gained, and is seen to be, not vain, but full of meaning. It is a way, indeed, which has certain similarities with nihilism, because it appears as a way into darkness and nothingness, and yet it is the one real opposite of nihilism: for it is life lived in the great affirmation, which never deceives, but fulfils all reasonable expectation, is itself fulfilment.

A decision about faith is to be expected at the point where every casual motive of action which accompanies faith breaks down and falls away, where pure faith is exposed to the test of confirmation, where it is deprived of all other powers and abandoned by them, and exposed, naked and defenceless, to their hostility. At this point, where there is nothing else attached to it, faith decides whether there is anything in it. Faith that is really faith knows that it is the victory which has conquered the world, in which the apparent superiority of the world is weakness and the apparent weakness of faith is the superior power. Faith and the power of faith, faith and the victory of faith are identical—even if they seem to the onlooker to be as widely separated as death and life, hell and heaven, nothingness and God.

When the meaning of power is so often distorted and abused, it is helpful to insist upon the clear distinction between questions of truth and right on the one hand, and of power on the other hand. But it would be a serious mistake to make a categorical separation of things that belong together. Though truth is often enough slandered and suppressed in one way or the other, it will only be taken seriously when its power is recognised and admitted, that is, its power to create its own validity and to establish itself. Something to which no kind of power can be entrusted cannot be called truth, just as lies steal their power from truth, and a lie which has been entirely exposed—that is, set in the light of the truth—is powerless. The same is true of right and righteousness, in the widest sense of what we have to recognise as morally good. Even if violence is done to the good a thousand times over, so long as we must acknowledge that it is good, that it is what is required and necessary and wholesome, we must continue to ascribe to it the power of the necessary and wholesome. And if we try to escape this despised power of the good, we find that we are persecuted by it in different disguises, and thus it takes its revenge upon us. When we are concerned with the true and the good, it would be better not to keep our distance from questions of power, but rather to be more thoroughly under the claim of the power of the true and good, that is, make it our responsibility to establish them effectively in history.

The same holds even more strongly of faith. To keep your distance from the question of its power, not to let it lay claim upon you, not to make use of faith's power, means to deny faith. For faith has to do with God. But one cannot speak of God without ascribing to him power over all power. Faith means participation in this omnipotence of God, because it is faith and nothing else which ascribes to him this power. If faith did not do this, it would not be done, and this power would be denied to God. Certainly, the common ascription of omnipotence to God has sunk to the level of a mere banality and a matter of course. This has little to do with faith, just as faith has little to do with such a supposed matter of course. For what does it mean to ascribe to God in this way the power over all power? Are we to think of physical power, raised to unimaginable intensity? Are we to think of human will-power, shorn of all limitations?

Whatever we attempt in this way, all we get is a ghost, which may make us shudder, but which we cannot take seriously. The relation of God's power to natural powers is not, in my view, part of the prolegomena of an understanding of faith, but belongs to a study of the last things. Similarly, the relation of God's power to man's will and his strivings, and thus to the strangely confused course of history, is at the end rather than the beginning of faith's knowledge of God's omnipotence. Certainly what faith recognises and confesses to be God's power involves a complete transformation in the common view of what power is. Where unbelief sees God's powerlessness, faith sees God's real and ultimate omnipotence. To faith the crucified witness of faith, in his surrender as the witness of God's love, is the very ground of faith. To confess God's omnipotence at the cross of Jesus is to know what omnipotence really is. " For the word of the cross is folly to those who are perishing, but to us who are being saved it is the power of God. . . . For the foolishness of God is wiser than men, and the weakness of God is stronger than men"(I Corinthians 1. 18, 25).

Hence the man who will not have his life based on Jesus is absolutely powerless. It would be misleading to illustrate this by the limits of his physical power and the corresponding limits of his knowledge. Certainly, his power even in these respects has its limits, in spite of its unimaginable extent. By certain standards it may even be called very restricted. But it would be foolish to deny or to belittle by spiteful comments the power which man in practice does have. We can only speak of man's powerlessness against the background of the unimaginable extent of his power. So we are not thinking of the greater or less extent of his power, but in the midst of all his power of a powerlessness which springs from his lack of faith, from his being dominated by unbelief. This is what the Bible describes as bondage to sin.

It would also be misleading to demonstrate man's real powerlessness by his being at the mercy of so-called fate, being only to a very limited extent master of his own decisions and able to carry out his plans, being in permanent uncertainty about the future and certain only that an end is set to his life, even if he succeeds in postponing it. For to be at the mercy of the hazards of life and death, however much it may remind us of man's ultimate powerlessness, is not, within the limits set for him, absolute powerlessness. We must therefore guard against exhibiting this simple powerlessness as a moral matter; as though mankind were one great morass, without the remarkable scale of moral possibilities in the life of each individual and in mankind as a whole. The moral misunderstanding of what the Bible describes as sin is one of the chief hindrances to an understanding of what faith really is. This does not mean that the powerlessness which is rooted in unbelief does not have effects in the moral sphere, as, for instance, in the incapacity for disinterested love.

We get nearer to man's absolute powerlessness when we reflect that he cannot change his past. In face of the future man is very largely powerless; in face of the past he is absolutely powerless. What has happened, has happened. What is broken, is broken. What has been omitted, has been omitted. But the pressure of what is past is not past, but all too present. And if it is dislodged from the present, then it enters the future, for it cannot be expunged from what we are and therefore will become. Yet how much has this powerlessness in face of our own past to do with unbelief? Clearly, we may speak of such a connection only if the powerlessness is not merely natural. But what is there here that is not just natural and inevitable slavery, but the slavery of guilt? Surely that I could be free, but will not. Not free *from* the past, by flight and oblivion, but free *for* the past, in bearing that which he who has been acquitted from the curse of the past is willing to bear. And thus free not only in face of the past, but also in face of the future; free not only in face of fate, but also in respect of my moral duties; not only in my relation to my neighbour, but also towards myself.

This unwillingness to admit that I could be free is paradoxically identical with the unwillingness to admit that I am simply powerless, that is, powerless in respect of myself, powerless to change, not this or that in myself, but my very self. I will not admit this profound powerlessness of mine. I think that I can be a self-asserting being with a right to itself and having itself, so to speak, in hand. Because I think in this way, and do not see that I am thrown upon God for him to come to my help against myself and free me from myself, and because at most I see myself as dependent on God for the completion and furtherance of my own self, the powerlessness of which I speak is deep-rooted, it will not accept help, it does not want to be free and therefore cannot be helped.

And yet it happens. The unbeliever believes, the man who is simply powerless shares in the omnipotence of God, the sinner is freed from himself. This is the happening which is a miracle in the strictest sense. Everything else that we might be inclined to describe as a miracle, and which might in fact be a miracle, is so only so far as it serves this one miracle of the divine grace, which can accomplish the incomprehensible, in making man free from himself. This is forgiveness, rebirth, justification. And it is at this point that we may understand God's omnipotence, as disclosing to one who is simply powerless the power of faith.

How does this miracle come about? Here is certainly a question of power: it is by the all-powerful grace of God, whose gracious choice cannot be fathomed or substantiated or criticised but only received. And yet the question how this miracle comes about, the way of this omnipotent grace, can be answered by pointing to how this miracle *has* happened, and from this one happening has opened a way to the ever new happening of the communication of faith from Jesus, by the preaching of the message to us.

Not less important than the question how this miracle comes about, is the question how it continues. Is this really a different question? The justification of the sinner, the unbeliever coming to believe, the powerless receiving power, the freeing of the slave —all this is a miracle. It can only remain a miracle, when the sinner, the unbeliever, the weak and the slave continues to live in this miracle, and that means, in faith, in sharing in God's omnipotence, and not in his own power and self-asserting freedom. If he wishes to remain in this miracle, then he will remain weak and a sinner, and, properly understood, will become ever more so, that is, will more and more have to acknowledge that God is right over against himself, more and more turn to God as the Lord of his life, more and more boast of his weakness, that God's power may be strong in this weakness.

This is the power of faith, that in virtue of God's love it comes to man and remains with him, which simply means that man has a different relation to God, the world, and himself. In what way different? One could simply say, in that he knows that he is loved. For faith comes from and goes to being loved. And with this has not everything happened that can be hoped for or demanded—all promises fulfilled, and the law fulfilled? Yes; when the event of faith has taken place, then basically everything has taken place. But much more takes place; on this basis of faith as being loved comes liberation from self-love. He who is loved by God no longer needs to love himself. He is free from this perversion of love. He is therefore free to love his neighbour. But all this—freedom from self-love, freedom to love one's neighbour—is the consequence, not the cause. They are mighty deeds of faith, not faith itself. As Luther says, " Faith is the doer, and love the deed " (WA 17, 2; 98).

XII

The Summons of Faith

On first glance the title of this lecture is obscure and enigmatic. What does it mean? What does it indicate? I intend it as a signpost or key for something that we think we know all about, and yet of which we have only the most confused notions, namely, what we commonly call the "church." There is a thick fog hanging over what the church really is. One cannot expect to make everything suddenly bright as noon by merely changing a word. It is of the nature of the matter that much in it should be obscure and confused. But where the darkness is so great, even a new word can give a little light.

At first I was inclined to adopt a more conventional title, such as " People of Faith " or " Community of Faith " or "Association of Faith " or " Fellowship of Faith." I was anxious to avoid any sensational or arbitrary high-lighting of a partial truth. I looked for a word that could interpret the manifold significance of "church" in the most comprehensive way, and could point in a direction that would be always helpful to remember. So I had to avoid the conventional words, and try to be bold. I got some inspiration from an Old Testament monograph that I was reading, and then some encouragement from a hymn that I remembered. So theology may be helped from modest sources. Further, some experience of the church, both persuasive and oppressive, combined to suggest this word, "summons," as particularly apt as a kind of compass for our reflection about the church. You cannot go far wrong, when hearing or speaking of the church, if you remember that it means a summons in matters of faith. Of course this needs further clarification both through reflection and practice. But first we must examine the reasons why the word "church," and the phenomenon it denotes, should be so confused.

The first reason is that the word "church" is inadequate to express the meaning of the New Testament word *ecclesia*. This is not necessarily due to the etymological provenance of "church," which is in any case almost buried, and not apparent in the current use of the word. The Greek word *ekklesia* has entered the Romance languages as a loan-word (*ecclesia, chiesa, église*), whereas in the Germanic languages (including English as well as German) the word *Kirche*, church, is derived, through the early encounter of Germanic tribes with Arian Christianity, from another Greek word, *kyriakon*, which means "belonging to the Lord." "Church" therefore is connected with *kyrios*, a title of honour which in the Greek translation of the Old Testament replaced the name of Jahweh and then in early Christianity came to be used exclusively for Jesus Christ. The adjective *kyriakos* thus came to mean "Christian." But while the direct Greek equivalent of our worn and tortured word "Christian," *christianos*, was used almost exclusively with reference to persons, namely, those who belonged to Christ, *kyriakos* was never used of persons, but solely of things: the Lord's Supper, the Lord's Day, the Lord's House. Each of these usages points indirectly to the meeting for the worship of God, not considered as the congregation, but pointing rather to the event, the time and the place where the congregation appears. "Church" would then be directly derived from the last of these meanings of *kyriakos*, namely, "the house of the Lord." Undoubtedly it makes good sense to understand the church as the property of Christ. But it may give rise to certain qualms, since it is not directly people but a building which is indicated as the property of Christ. And from this comes the further use of the word "church" to indicate something static and institutional. This tendency can even be seen in the New Testament, where *ekklesia* is sometimes compared to a building (a building in course of being built) and to a temple. And if we mean by "church" at any place primarily the building, we could always understand this as the visible indication of an *event* which is continually taking place there, namely, the gathering of the worshipping congregation.

The difficulties with the word, then, arise not so much from etymology as from the history of the word itself. So far as we are not thinking of the church building, we mean by church an organisation and an institution, in distinction from the local congregation. We cannot help thinking of the church as an association of local congregations, of a structure which is built up over the congregations, of a whole consisting of many parts. Yet all this completely misses the point of the New Testament way of speaking of the *ekklesia*. For the Greek word includes in one what we separate into the local congregation on the one hand, and the whole church on the other hand; even when, in English, we use the word "church" for both conceptions, we use it in the two different senses. There is still another usage, which is quite absent from the New Testament, when we use neutral, purely sociological language to denote churches as confessions or denominations competing with one another in their teachings and struggle with one another for room in the world.

In New Testament usage the *ekklesia* is essentially one. But it is of the very nature of this one *ekklesia* that it should appear in many *ekklesiai*. Wherever the *ekklesia* appears, it does so as the one *ekklesia*, and not just as a part of it. Both the so-called local church, whether the *ekklesia* in Corinth or Jerusalem or Rome, and even the gathering of Christians in a house-church, and the whole church of Christ in all places, are described by the same word. We can get at the sense of this only by giving up the common double terminology, and either always translate *ekklesia* by "church," even when we are speaking just of a house-church, or always translate it by congregation, even when we mean the whole church of Christ. Yet even then the real aim would not be reached. For the concepts church and congregation have been formed precisely as complementary, so that we cannot avoid having misleading ideas and questions about them. If we had to choose, then it would be preferable to translate *ekklesia* throughout by "congregation," since the idea of a concrete gathering undoubtedly clings to it. On the other hand, it would be quite wrong to give currency to the view that this congregation of Christ was originally just the concrete individual congregation, and that it was only a later development which turned to the idea of the whole, in the sense of a union in a higher unity. On the contrary, the standpoint of the whole, of an indivisible unity, is primary to the concept of the *ekklesia*, not, indeed, in the sense of an organisation, but of a new creation.

The historical development of the church, and the changes this has brought about in the style of life of the *ekklesia*, make it extraordinarily difficult to understand the New Testament view properly. We have to try and free ourselves of our ideas of structure and organisation, of the whole and its parts, and think only of what constitutes the reality of the *ekklesia*, quite apart from the place, the nature and the extent of its representation. Perhaps the best way to bring it home to us is to consider the dogma of the presence of the whole Christ in the whole host as in each of its parts. " For where two or three are gathered in my name, there am I in the midst of them "(Matthew 18.20). But notice that this is true of every gathering in the name of Jesus Christ.

There is yet another reason in the history of the word *ekklesia* why the word "church" should prevent us from seeing something quite decisive. Originally *ekklesia* was a secular word, which meant an assembly of the people: not an arbitrary collection, but an assembly of the people which had been properly summoned by the herald. When the church described itself it did not make use of one of the various possible religious expressions of the time, such as were customarily used to describe religious and cultic associations. Christianity did not regard itself as a new establishment in the purely religious realm, which even then was characterised by rich and varied propaganda and competition among pious societies and religious clubs with every possible variety of promise and invitation. Of the available words the most suitable was that which denoted the regular assembly of the people: a secular, public, legal gathering, with something exclusive about it. There could be many religious associations in one place, but only one such assembly of the people.

This word *ekklesia*, however, was not taken over casually, for it had already had a place in the Greek translation of the Old Testament, where the frequent description of the people of Israel as the "congregation of God" was translated by *ekklesia*. Christianity regarded itself as the legitimate continuation of this people of God, as the true Israel, as the congregation of the new covenant. But although it was determinative that this was *God's* people, an assembly called into being by *God*, by a summons of *God*, the Old Testament made no distinction between the religious and the profane, the "church" and the world. Admittedly, the identification which was characteristic of Israel between the congregation of the people and the congregation of God, even though it suffered from constant tensions, was broken by Christianity. But there are two main symptoms which indicate that we cannot suitably speak of the Christian congregation being restricted to the purely religious realm, but must rather regard it as something entirely *sui generis* and unprecedented—that the community of faith, in other words, is something different from a religious community.

The first symptom is that what was from the religious standpoint an impassable barrier, namely, the difference between Jew and non-Jew, was in fact overcome. The deeply rooted religious tendency to particularity, to separation, to being distinguished as something better in the division between the pure and the impure, the privileged and the unprivileged, the haves and the have-nots, was abolished. In its stead the opposite tendency was at work, to invite all without limitation, to exclude nobody, who does not exclude himself, to permit no distinction of persons, which is abolished in the context of faith, and would appear there as meaningless and as a purely natural and worldly phenomenon. " There is neither Jew nor Greek, there is neither slave nor free, there is neither male nor female, for you are all one in Christ Jesus" (Galatians 3.28). But this does not mean one in the sense of a general unification such as would arise by the levelling of all differences—that is a utopian notion—but in the sense of the opening up of a new possibility, in face of which all traditional alternatives are unimportant. For ultimately, that is, before God, we know that everyone is in the same position: all are impure, and all become pure before God solely by faith, without any special religious work. This is something so entirely different, cutting across all religions, that it helps to show how the community of faith is something different from a religious community.

The second symptom is connected with the first. Christianity lacked what was then an essential part of a religion. There were no priests and no sacrifice. The crucified Jesus, raised to the right hand of God, is the only "priest" (but we can only use the word "priest" in quotation marks), and this marks the end of all priesthood. His death is the once-for-all sufficient "sacrifice" (again in quotation marks), which deprives all sacrificial cults of their

meaning. So we can also turn the traditional religious terminology round, and abolish it in another way, by saying that all are
now "priests" who believe in Jesus Christ. In faith they present
their bodies, that is, themselves, as a living "sacrifice," holy and
acceptable to God. That is their reasonable worship (cf. Romans
12.1). Certainly, Christians assemble together to worship God.
But this cannot be called a cultic act, any more than baptism is a
rite of initiation or the Lord's Supper a festive meal of the kind
found in the mystery religions. Rather, in all these things the one
thing is intended to be proclaimed, made clear, and recalled again
and again, in common confession and practice, namely, that with
Jesus there is opened up the faith which is the end of all religious
fear and all religious works, because it is peace with God, acceptance as the sons of God, participation in his omnipotence,
and freedom from the curse of the law in the certainty of
salvation.

This consciousness that Christianity was completely different
from all religion was expressed in the conviction that they were
a community of the last days, that they were partakers of the
kingdom of God, which was already breaking in, and that they
were the first of a new humanity. There were still clinging to
these ideas it is true, a good many religious thought-forms which
had been split asunder by the message of faith, the gospel of Jesus
Christ. And it is not surprising that ·the understanding of faith
threatened to be submerged again by a religious self-understanding which re-introduced the whole religious paraphernalia of
priests and cult and religious performances; and, in fact, turned
faith into the Christian religion. For this tendency is so powerful
that it cannot be eradicated by means of outer reforms, the abolition of priests and masses and monasteries. Even where Christianity exists in the form of religion and under the law of religion,
the witness to Christ can produce true faith; while on the
other hand, to surrender this kind of religious form does not in

the least mean the elimination of the structure of what we specifically mean by religion, namely, care about oneself, self-assertion before God, the desire to give God something, instead of simply receiving everything from him. This perversion, which seeks religious achievements, this Christian piety which replaces justifying faith, is deeply rooted in Protestantism as well. And the reformation of which the church is always in need does not consist so much of the removal of defects, the rousing of the sleepy, taking the divine commands seriously, and so on. These are all consequences, in the proper course of events; and if they take place without faith they are no more than changes on the surface. The one and only reformation which the church always stands in need of is faith. In respect of religion this means taking seriously the fact that we can give to God only that which he already has—his honour, and that this honour is his mercy, and that therefore God can only be honoured by faith.

It has become very difficult indeed to understand the word "church" in the sense I have tried to elaborate. The church has become a religious concept for us, in contradistinction to the realm of the profane. The opposition of the church and the world as two different empirical concepts can hardly be avoided. The word "church" is thus in danger of concealing the very truth it is meant to express. It is not surprising that "the church" is extended to denote the general idea of a religious species, which then needs the addition of the word "Christian," in order to make clear which church is meant.

A third and last reason for the far-reaching confusion in the idea of the church is the image of the actual phenomenon of the church. Here we find innumerable different points of view, as well as a whole series of complaints and criticisms of the church, which have become commonplaces: the divisions in Christendom, with each church imprisoned in its own tradition and full of self-righteousness, the dogmatism and intellectualism of theology, the love of power among ecclesiastical leaders, the indolence and apathy of the laity, the clinging to the past, the remoteness of sermons from reality, the grotesque efforts on the part of the church to reach the significant groups in modern society, the workers, the intellectuals, and so on. In this catalogue I merely give an indication of what could be extended in innumerable variations. Let us leave it now. Not because it can be hushed up or glossed over—on the contrary; there must be intensive analysis and criticism of the historical development of the church, as well as of its present condition, so that we may have an impression of the fearful disbalance between the real nature of the church and the actual phenomenon. Is the church, as we know it among us to-day, even remotely challenging men to a decision? In the conflict between east and west has it shown the liberating authority which may contribute something towards breaking the vicious circle of fear and threat? Is the church really able and willing to help the so-called under-developed nations, which are nevertheless developing with such immense speed? Critical reflections of this sort are fruitful only if we keep in view the really critical point, and go to the root of the matter. We must not stop short at the symptoms, but must speak positively of the church as the summons to faith.

How much does this help? Does it really point the way? At any rate, it makes it clear that the important thing is the togetherness of men who have been reached by the message of faith, who are called and claimed, and form a unity. This unity does not mean a uniform organisation. But where the word of faith is heard, the summons becomes acute, there men are gathered together and enter upon a movement which, however different the place and the time and the circumstances, is the one movement, since it is a summons in the name of faith. Further, this personal character of the summons is not the whole story. Men do not come together in order to enjoy the fellowship, far less to exhibit themselves as believers. Rather, they are answering a call which surpasses all individual interest, and all community interest based on individuals. There is something more at stake than is given in the formula, "the community of the faithful." What is at stake is faith itself, and that means what Jesus Christ stands for: the summons to believe, in which each individual is just a serving member. He who answers this summons is not doing his own work, but as the instrument of God is doing God's work. Hence the summons to believe is a sending into a crisis, a movement into an event which we cannot command. The summons looks to the future, "which has already begun," as we may rightly say in view of the battle which is already raging. But we must guard against martial sounds, the clattering of weapons and the consciousness of one's powers, as though they were appropriate here. For this summons is not just for the young and strong, but also for old men, for women and children, not just for the highly educated, but also for the simple and uncomplicated, not just for those of moral integrity, but also for the morally frail and broken. It is a strange collection, which cannot make much of a parade or win any brilliant victories. But this is the mystery of this summons, that the weak and frail may often do more than the strong and imposing. For in the summons of faith every capacity and skill is relativised by the power of faith.

That this summons is a summons *to believe* is the reason why we have been able to insert this discussion of the church. For in reflecting what this summons to believe means we are able to cast light on the problem of the church. I suggest two further points which can guide us on the way.

First, if we still ask why the church is necessary at all, then we have not grasped what faith is. Admittedly, the question whether the church is necessary is secondary. For the first thing is that faith has to do with the summons that comes in Jesus' name. You cannot believe unless you submit to this summons. For to believe and to share in the work of God, which is directed to all men, are one and the same thing. If this summons were not there before we were, then the call to faith would not have reached us. And this call to faith would not have reached us at all unless the summons to faith were passed on by us. Unless there is obedience to this summons, and action upon it, faith cannot be faith. For this is the power of faith of which we spoke, that it brings about obedience to the summons.

Second, we have not grasped what the church is until we see all that can be said, expected and experienced of it, from the point of view of the summons of faith. The church is the summons to believe. That is how the worship of the church is to be regarded —so that we do not leave as those who are dismissed, but as those who have a summons and a sending. And that is the meaning of the service given by those who dedicate their lives to the service of the church: it is service in the summons of faith. So too with the so-called laity: they are summoned to believe. This is the simple criterion for what is important, what unimportant, what is necessary and what superfluous, what is to be done and what omitted in the church, what must be taken up and what must be changed. It is a revolutionary criterion. For what minister, and congregation, and church authorities, and individual Christian would not have to revolutionise their thoughts in many different respects, if they took this criterion seriously? But at the same time this criterion is an excellent safeguard. For it provides liberation from the restlessness of programmes of reform. In face of this criterion all the endlessly discussed problems of the church fall into the background—problems of church order and form, of established church or free church, of wider responsibility to the public as against concentration on the inner community, of more elaborate liturgies as against more practical works. The real question which remains is whether, no matter the forms, the summons of faith is heard at all. And to-day this means that in a conjunction of sobriety and imagination the demon of *Angst* should be overcome, and real authority, not the pseudo-authority of violence, should reign along with selfless love. And this, if anything, is what the world expects, and has a right to expect, from the church.

XIII

The Sphere of Faith

Justification by faith alone, according to Reformed teaching, is not one doctrine beside many others, but constitutes the whole of Christian faith. It is not just one side of it, far less a one-sided view which has to be completed, by, say, sanctification. Nor does the doctrine of justification place an undue emphasis upon the individual, with his sense of guilt and his longing for salvation, with the consequent need for a corrective through greater emphasis on the so-called last things, so neglected by the Reformation and so beloved of the sects: all the events that are still to come, Christ's second coming, the reign of a thousand years, and so on. Justification by faith alone is not an object of faith, but the very reality of faith. It defines faith itself, not a partial aspect of it. If faith alone justifies, then no completion of Reformed doctrine is possible. If completion and correction are thought necessary, then Reformed teaching is in effect abolished. Justifying faith does not have sanctification or faith in the last things alongside it. But if these themes really concern Christian faith—and who would dispute it?—then they are to be found in justifying faith itself, as an explication of its meaning. Though apparently independent and additional themes, they are properly handled as expositions of justifying faith. Only in this way can their connection with faith be clearly seen. Nor is this just a discovery of theologians, whose job is to systematise. The question is rather whether we grasp the one thing necessary. The Christian proclamation, when it really knows what it is about, is not like a shop offering all kinds of goods for sale, according to need and taste. But it proclaims the one thing that is absolutely necessary. The one who is absolutely necessary is God. And that is why—not despite this or in addition to it—faith alone is what is absolutely necessary. For "the two belong together, faith and God," as Luther says in his *Large Catechism* (WA 30, 1; 133). If it is to be properly understood and carry conviction, the Christian proclamation must not have many things to say, but only the one thing.

In the course of our exposition we spoke of justification by faith alone under the theme of "the reality of faith." It is in line with what I said in my introduction that we have not let this theme out of sight, and now in the conclusion of the whole matter still hold fast to it. All the other subjects we have discussed are subsidiary to it. So it was with the power of faith and the summons of faith. And the present subject, the sphere of faith, is also to be regarded as a more precise formulation of the question about the reality of faith.

This question asks where faith is to be met, where, one might say, it is essentially present. But immediately the question begins to shimmer and change, under the influence of certain insidious ideas and interests. Thus the question might be taken to refer to the sphere where faith is possible. This change in the formulation does not necessarily lead us astray. But it is misleading if it assumes that there is a particular place, the place of faith, where one must go in order to be able to believe. The question then implies that we must look around for a signpost leading us to the land of faith. And this in turn implies the view that there must first be a change in me before I can believe. This change as a precondition of faith is regarded as a change in the circumstances of my life. This attitude could be interpreted thus: I should

certainly like to believe, but the place where I at present am is
not at all a place of faith. So I long for a place which makes faith
possible.

There is another variation, similar to the last. It could be
expressed thus: we have heard enough about the nature of faith.
We now have a fair idea of what it is. But now the one interesting
thing which is still to be answered is where this faith is really to
be found. This rather uncomfortable question cannot be dismissed as fundamentally a wrong question. But the question is
wrongly put, if it implies that faith can be described apart from
the sphere of faith, and that to describe it in its purity you must
eliminate the question about the sphere of faith. For—the implication runs—since the place where a thing is affects its relation
to and its contact with other things, faith can be defined in its
purity only when it is disentangled from the rest of reality. So it
is supposed that where faith is encountered in reality it can *eo
ipso* not be pure faith, but is mixed with alien things, and is bound
to be compromised.

In resolute opposition to this idea of an ideal perfection of being
and unhappy imperfection of reality, the question about the sphere
of faith must be seen as a question about its reality: only in this
way is its nature truly illuminated. It is impossible to define faith
in its purity, apart from this question about where it is. It can
only be defined with regard to its place. The more one tries to
represent it in abstraction from where it is, the more its lines are
blurred by alien elements. And the more one allows the question
of its place to dominate, the more purely does faith appear. For
faith lives not in the abstract, the general and the timeless, but in
the concrete, the particular and the historical. That is why the
question about the sphere of faith is so helpful, for it indicates
that a proper grasp of faith depends on its connections and
relations with others. Faith is by nature something lived, not
thought, it is an event, not an idea. It does not *have* being, but

it *is*. So the answer to the question, where faith is, is that it is in time. Time is the sphere of faith.

This may still sound rather obscure. So I add that the world is the sphere of faith, which is, rightly understood, the same as to say that its sphere is time. This must now be elaborated in opposition to various objections and misinterpretations.

First, there is the prevalent view that it is not the world, but rather the world beyond, or the transcendent, which is the sphere of faith; and that faith is thorough and logical when it cuts itself off from the world and turns wholly to the transcendent. Burning its bridges to this world, it is really no longer here, but has left this life behind, if not in inspired ecstasy, at least in longing anticipation of the change of sphere which is proper to faith. There is a powerful stream of Christian linguistic tradition which seems to mean something of this sort. None less than St. Paul says, " My desire is to depart and be with Christ." And so long as this departure is still to take place, at least it has been regarded as the ideal, though indeed without the authority of St. Paul, who also knew that to remain in the flesh was more necessary on account of others. There is all the same this sharp antithesis, which we hear again in St. Paul's words to the Galatians, how through the cross of Christ "the world has been crucified to me and I to the world" (Galatians 6.14). What appears to be the *locus classicus* for this view that faith is not located in the world is I John 2.15ff., " Do not love the world or the things in the world. If any one loves the world, love for the Father is not in him. For all that is in the world, the lust of the flesh and the lust of the eyes and the pride of life, is not of the Father but is of the world. And the world passes away, and the lust of it; but he who does the will of God abides for ever."

Must we then say that the world is at most the sphere of faith in the sense that it is faith's starting-point, from which it flees from the world? There is so much Christian witness pointing in this direction that one cannot simply reject it as a time-conditioned misunderstanding, happily left behind by, for instance, a Protestantism which is open to the world. For, as is well known, in Protestantism, this "happy" achievement is very quickly succeeded by the hangover of extreme pessimism about civilisation. The popular alternative of flight from the world or openness to the world has to be rejected as involving misunderstandings on both sides. For example, it is very doubtful whether the cheap Protestant criticism of monasticism as a flight from the world can really be justified. Even in that extreme form of ascetic flight from the world, the life of the hermit, the desert was chosen as the sphere of faith just because in its solitude the world was most fearfully present in its demonic power. And so faith had to live its life there, in conflict. We might indeed ask whether on such a view the world as the sphere of faith is properly understood, and indeed whether the world and faith, here found in mutual dependence, are really properly involved. This question becomes all the more pressing when we consider the Gnostic understanding of the world and the self, in which the view of the world as a cosmos, in which the Greeks rejoiced, was transformed into an experience of the world as an unavoidable fate, from which men could only be saved by being taken completely out of the world. Whereas for the Greeks the world itself, properly understood, was salvation, for the Gnostics salvation consisted of liberation from the world, and the destruction of its nothingness. It is possible to see in this Gnostic view, in a striking form, a decisive trait of Christian faith, namely, the sovereign freedom of faith from the world.

And yet it is precisely the wrong way taken by Gnosticism which reminds us of the immovable limit which has to be respected even in the sharpest formulation of the antithesis between faith and the world, if it still claims to be Christian. Faith affirms the world as the creation of God. It confesses Jesus

Christ as Lord and Saviour not just of a little group of "spiritual" people who have been liberated from the world, but of the whole world. The love of God which is revealed in the sending of Christ means that God loved the *world* (John 3.16)—an affirmation which stands boldly beside the injunction, "Do not love the world." So we must just as boldly interpret this warning to mean "Love the world, because God loves it; love it in the way he does." For how can he love the Creator who does not love the creation? How can one confess and praise God as Creator, and deny and hate his work? But before we unite these contradictory affirmations of faith about the world in the one affirmation that the world is the place of faith, let us look at some other considerations with which this affirmation seems to conflict.

It is said that the church is the sphere of faith, and the church is opposed to the world. Here, too, in regard to this subject of the church and the world, the tradition is rich. Nor can it be disputed that faith and the church go together. For as we have already made clear, the church is the summons to faith. It *is* this event of faith. That is why it is inadvisable to speak of the church as the sphere of faith. Certainly, the individual believer belongs to this summons, and to that extent has his place in it, he sees himself in a certain respect as carried along by it, as protected by it, claimed and given his duties. But it always proves fatal to allow this view of the church to dominate as the sphere where faith is to be found. For if the church is properly interpreted as the summons to faith, then the question about the sphere of faith is identical with that about the sphere of the church, the sphere of this summons. Then the only answer is the lapidary interpretation of the parable of the weeds in the field: "The field is the world" (Matthew 13.38).

It is pious talk, but all the same just superficial jargon, to say that the church is opposed to the world. It is true that this may often be just an unfortunate way of saying that the church does not come from the world, but that it offers something in the world that is not of the world. But this must be understood as meaning being for the world. If only those who are so quick with this opposition of the church and the world would take their bearings from him who is the ground of faith and the Head of 'the church and the model of the Christian attitude to the world! He sat with sinners at the same table, he ate from the same bowl as Judas, and bore witness to God's love for the world on the cross. Here we may see what it means to let the world be the sphere of faith. Certainly it means an opposition as between light and darkness, when a light shines in a dark place, as when Christ says, " I am the light of the world " (John 8.12), or in the summons to faith, " You are the light of the world " (Matthew 5.14). But this is the paradoxical opposition of the light to the dark place where it shines, that it gives itself to this darkness, that its light is for the place where it shines.

A light that is a light for itself is a contradiction. Light is for others, its life is to light up the place where it is. In precisely the same way a church is a contradiction which is, if not solely, at least chiefly, there for itself, taken up with its self-limitation, self-preservation and self-assertion, concerned to be distinguished from the world by occupying a piece of the world which it cultivates as a spiritual realm distinct from the worldly realm. This tendency not to allow the world to be the sphere of faith, but to mark off a special sphere from the world as the sphere of the church and of faith—that is, the tendency to sanctify a piece of the world, —leads to the opposite danger, that of the holy being made worldly. We might put it in a sentence: to clericalise the world is just a special form of secularising the church. And a great deal of anti-modernist effort to-day, which is regarded by its protagonists as a de-secularising, is likewise just a variant of secularisation. Beside, all such drawing of the line between "the sphere of the church" and "the sphere of the world" is bound to go wrong.

One speaks, for instance, of saints, but one cannot hold to the New Testament usage, that all believers, *as believers*, are saints. That this model of the church against the world is a false starting-point may be gauged from the fact that this opposition of the two is made part of a pious ideology and edifying manner of speaking which gets on pretty well with the world. But when there is a question of serious opposition between the two you meet with surprise and indignation.

I am aware that my remarks are provocative, and not safe-guarded by any qualifications. It would certainly be necessary to remember that the church must claim space, and time, and money, and so on. All that is a part of the fact that its sphere is the world. But everything depends on the right criterion for these claims and for this use of the world by the church. The criterion comes from the point where we ask in how far the world is the sphere of faith.

One final objection must be taken up. Does our way of putting it not compete with the other and more obvious way, that Christ is the sphere of faith? Surely this usage is deeply rooted in Christian message, that he who has come to believe is now in Christ, and that therefore faith's place is in Christ. But we spoke of Christ as the ground of faith. The ground of faith is that from which faith receives its life. The sphere of faith, on the other hand, is where faith lives its life. We must notice the connection between these two assertions: not although, but because, faith is based on Christ, its sphere is the world. This is indicated by all the sayings which describe the summons of faith as a sending into the world (" like sheep among wolves," Matthew 10.16). And in the so-called high-priestly prayer we hear explicitly: " I do not pray that thou shouldst take them out of the world, but that thou shouldst keep them from the evil one. They are not of the world, even as I am not of the world. . . . As thou didst send me into the world, so I have sent them into the world " (John 17.15f., 18). Since the church is called the body of Christ, in which we are made members by faith, we are promised participation in Christ's mission to the world, his way in the world, his life for the world. Faith as the following of Jesus has the world as its sphere.

This does not mean that faith now has certain duties imposed upon it, which it has to perform as best it may, as though faith were in the first instance simply faith and then had an additional mission to fulfil in the world, which has to be carried out as the requisite following of Christ. This might seem so obvious as not to need discussion. Yet there is something very important at stake here. We have already seen how it is impossible to determine what faith is unless we take account of where it is. Now we must put the matter the other way round, and say that the sphere of faith, the world, is not seen for what it is, if it is regarded merely as a mission field. Of course, this needs more detailed working out. But we must never forget that faith can only be faith in the world; not just because the commission to the world is so much a part of the nature of faith that it cannot be neglected—true though this is—but above all, because if faith did not have the world it would have lost its object.

This is again very provocative language. Are we to say, then, that the world is the object of faith? Should this object not rather be God and Christ and all the other articles of faith that one could enumerate? The idea of the object of faith is indeed so firmly tied to this way of thinking that any effort to struggle against it is probably useless. Yet I must try to make this point clear. Faith is not established by the intellectual appropriation of certain objects of consciousness; but faith is established on the ground of faith. An object of faith in the traditional sense can only be this ground of faith, and the witness to it. To cling to this with all one's life is what makes faith. Yet I consider it an unfortunate description to call this "the object of faith," since this gives rise to the fateful notion of a certain number of articles of faith which have to be mastered and laboriously acquired. Let us abandon this idea of an object of faith, in favour of the "material" of faith. Fichte once described the world as the material of duty. When I now speak of the world as the material of faith, I do not mean that it is the material for the duties of faith. No doubt faith has many tasks in the world. But the world as the material of faith does not in the first instance mean something like the works and fruits of faith; but it is in the very realm of the nature of faith. This nature consists in its mastering the world, in having in the world at once its material, its object, its opposition and thus its concrete reality. What do we mean when we say, " I believe in God the Father"—or in Christ, or in the Holy Spirit? Of course these are specific confessions and doctrines, which have a necessary connection with faith. But you can only have actual, concrete faith in concrete situations, that is, in face of, in holding out and taking your stand against, all that is standing in your way and contradicting the belief that God is your Father, that Jesus is the Christ, and that the Holy Spirit has been poured out. Faith that is not attacked and tempted is not faith at all. For faith can only be present where it says "nevertheless," and where it is realised in the concrete circumstances of your life. And this holds true of its intellectual formulation as well. When faith is described in Hebrews 11.1 as "the assurance of things hoped for," then its sphere is clearly where something opposes this hope. And when faith is further described as "the conviction of things not seen," again its sphere is where our eyes, and not just our eyes, meet with fearful barriers. It would be folly to say that faith's sphere is where one sees nothing. Rather, its sphere is where one sees a great deal, so terribly much that one involuntarily closes one's eyes, because the sight is unendurable. But faith does not believe because it closes its eyes. Rather, faith means to hold and trust, with eyes that see, to what one does not see: to hope against hope, to believe against experience.

This means, further, that faith is not a separate act, a kind of speculative soaring into transcendence. But it determines existence as existence in this world, and thus it is not something alongside all that I do and suffer, hope and experience, but something that is concretely present in it all, that is, it determines all my doing and suffering, hoping and experiencing. Faith has been turned into a separate work alongside other works, or it has been abstractly separated from them. If faith concerns man's personal being, if it decides who I am before God (that is, one with whom God is), then it includes all that I am, and is related to it all. This is the great thing to be learned, that faith has to be lived not as something in itself, but in concrete existence.

It should now be clear that, because the world is the sphere of faith, we can also say that time is the sphere of faith. For this is what the world means: the world which concerns and meets me in concrete situations, the world which can be characterised as temporal and historical. If you do not let the world concern you, and that means, if you take no notice of what is happening now, and are not open to the fact that everything has its time; if you do not notice the difference in the times, and thus flee from the sphere of faith—in this way you may indeed have a timeless relation to the ideas of faith; but they will be the ideas of yesterday. And this is not faith. This kind of general availability of ideas of faith is an abstraction from history. It is time alone which determines faith in its confession of " I believe."

But should we not turn everything round and say that only faith can be concerned with the world, only faith notices what is happening now, only faith is really open to the fact that everything has its time, only faith notices the difference in the times? Must one not say that faith alone makes the world into the sphere of faith? And must one not go a step farther and ask the somewhat odd question: What is the sphere of the world, and the sphere of time, that the world and time can be the sphere of faith? To this I should like to give the equally odd reply, that the sphere of the world and of time, the sphere where the world is encountered as the world, where it is experienced as the world, the sphere where time presses upon us and is received as time, abused or gained, this sphere where such important things happen that the world and time are decided in them, is the conscience. Because the world is the sphere of faith, conscience has in fact to do with faith. For only when faith makes the conscience free, and takes possession of it, can the conscience allow the world and time to be themselves.

In conclusion, faith makes the world what it truly is, the creation of God. It rids the world of demons and myths, and lets it again be what God wills it to be. Because faith frees us from the world, it frees us for the world. Because it does not live on the world, it makes it possible for us to live for the world. Because it puts an end to the misuse of the world, it opens the way to the right use of the world. Because it breaks the domination of the world, it gives domination over it and responsibility for it. And because it drives out the liking and the misliking of the world, it creates room for pure joy in the world.

XIV

The Steadfastness of Faith

Our question about faith led us to ask about its reality, then about its sphere, which is the world, or more precisely, time. In all this we felt more and more compelled not to consider faith in the abstract or for itself, but concretely, in its relation to the whole of reality. We must go still further in this direction. We must now speak explicitly of the being of faith here and now in the world and time. That is, we must speak of the life and way of faith, of its actual happening. The first theme, the "history of faith," must be taken up again, this time in less broad outlines, and in greater concentration on the temporal life of faith. And when I say that this actual life of faith must be expressed as the steadfastness of faith, I mean that it is by no means a matter of course that faith should continue to be. It is rather a miracle that faith should continue and endure. Faith endures because it is threatened, called in question, and tempted. This is of the very substance of faith. It is not additional or accidental, a mere misfortune of faith, which normally happens, but by the proper norm of faith should not happen. Rather, this threat and question directed to faith, this tempting of faith, is of its very nature. Faith would not be alive with its own proper life if it were not exposed to temptation. Faith without temptation is dead. Living faith is tempted faith.

This certainly contradicts the prevalent conception of faith. On this view temptation means the end or at least the reduction of faith. And faith is considered to be more alive and pure in proportion as it is unshakably and triumphantly lifted above all temptation. This is not meant to deny, but rather to presuppose, that faith is a fighting matter, and that its life is a struggle. But there is a difference between trivialising this fight, and escaping from it as far as possible, and seeing that faith is in deadly peril, where any negligence could spell its end. Faith would cease to be faith if it were not threatened.

It is not only the Old Testament, especially the Psalms and the Book of Job, which provides moving witness to the profound relationship between faith and temptation. In the New Testament, too, this note can be heard, more strongly, perhaps, than one might suppose. The figure of Jesus would be turned into an imaginary idealised image if there were lacking that trait which is indicated by the Temptation stories, Gethsemane, and the cry of dereliction on the cross: "My God, my God, why hast thou forsaken me?" (Matthew 27.46). And it is just at this point that the Epistle to the Hebrews sees the significance of Jesus for our salvation: "For we have not a high priest who is unable to sympathise with our weaknesses, but one who in every respect has been tempted as we are, yet without sinning. . . . For because he himself has suffered and been tempted, he is able to help those who are tempted." We recall, further, the words ascribed to Jesus by the Gospel according to St. Luke, directly before his passion: "Simon, Simon, behold, Satan demanded to have you, that he might sift you like wheat, but I have prayed for you, that your faith may not fail . . ." (Luke 22.31f.). St. Paul, too, has the same thing to say: "Therefore let any one who thinks that he stands take heed lest he fall. No temptation has overtaken you that is not common to man. God is faithful, and he will not let you be tempted beyond your strength, but with the temptation will also provide the way of escape, that you may be able to endure it" (I Corinthians 10.12f.). And he describes the life of believers as hidden beneath antitheses: "as impostors, and yet true; as unknown, and yet well known; as dying, and behold we live; as punished, and yet not killed; as sorrowful, yet always rejoicing; as poor, yet making many rich; as having nothing, and yet possessing everything" (II Corinthians 6.8-10).

What this means for the life of faith is very largely unregarded. No one has seen the indivisible connection between faith and temptation so clearly as Luther. This indeed is the point of the first of his famous Ninety-five Theses, where he says that it is the will of Christ that the whole life of the believer should consist of "penitence." And penitence means to be exposed to accusations, to wrath, to pain, to execution. And the life of faith is a life in baptism, and baptism means dying and rising again. "This meaning, the dying or drowning of sin," says Luther, "is not perfectly fulfilled in this life, till man also dies physically and becomes dust. The sacrament or sign of baptism is soon over, as we watch it, but its meaning, spiritual baptism, the drowning of sin, lasts as long as we live, and is completed only in death. Then a man is truly immersed in baptism, and there takes place what baptism means. Hence the whole of this life is nothing but a spiritual baptism going on unceasingly till death. And he who is baptized is condemned to death. . . . The sooner a man dies after his baptism, the sooner will his baptism be completed. . . . So the life of a Christian is nothing but a beginning to a blessed death, from his baptism to his grave" (WA 2; 728).

But we have still to discuss the nature of the temptation which is thus claimed to be a very part of faith. But first an observation which is fundamental to any talk about faith at all. It is not easy to put it into words, yet it concerns the success or failure of our whole effort to describe the nature of faith. At least it ought by now to be clear that faith is not to be described and communicated as a system of thought. It ought rather to be clear that faith is an event, but not, as is so often said, a spiritual event taking place in the inwardness of the believing subject, but an event taking place in relation between the existing person and that which is outside himself, namely, God. And this relation of man to God is at the same time, in the self-understanding of faith, a relation of God to man: so faith is an event which takes place between man and the whole of reality which concerns him. In faith the being of man between God and the world is determined.

But what precisely is the meaning of faith as an event? Even when this description is wholeheartedly affirmed, there is still the possibility of a fundamental misunderstanding. We must indeed reckon with the fact that it is a very prevalent misunderstanding. It arises when the event of faith is described and systematised in biographical form. First, man's situation is depicted without faith, in his sin and lost condition, and this discloses the reason why man is thrown back upon faith. Then we have a description of how the knowledge of his condition arises in the man, and at the same time his readiness for faith; and so his conversion from unbelief to faith takes place. Finally, we have a description of life in this state of faith, in which faith is active in producing fruits, though the believer experiences all sorts of setbacks, and can even fall away from faith. But faith remains something whole and complete in itself, and the aim is to hold fast to it and to prove it.

In such an outline of faith the real event is its arising, its coming to be; that is, the arising of a condition or an ability. When this is applied to concrete circumstances there are two possibilities. Either you regard faith as being founded in a single event, a more or less precisely datable conversion, or you regard it as a series of individual acts, arising anew. In each case faith comes into being as the realisation of something prescribed and traced out beforehand, which is always the same and at every moment of its existence is something complete and entire.

Now this basic outline, and its two concrete applications, have grasped something essential. The decisive thing in the event of faith is indeed its arising, that is, the turning from unbelief to faith. And this must always determine anything else that we have to say about faith. The event of faith is to be interpreted as the constant arising of faith in so far as faith is always accompanied by unbelief, and can only be truly faith at the point where unbelief has been defeated. And if by penitence, in this basic outline, is meant the arising of faith, then life as permanent penitence means this permanent arising of faith. Clearly this view contradicts the conception of conversion as a single and once-for-all event. Yet one must not disregard the truth in this view: for there is in faith this once-for-allness. Faith knows that it is grounded in the once-for-all event of Christ, which has once for all changed the situation of the whole world. Faith knows that it has been handed over to this event of Christ in the once-for-all and unrepeatable event of baptism, and that no falling away can cancel this. Moreover, the uniqueness of the event of Christ, as of the event of baptism, are clearly connected with the unique and unrepeatable nature of human life. Each of us is born once, and never again. Each of us must die, some day, and no one can rehearse this, or reverse it. Every moment of our life, from birth to death, happens once, and can neither be revoked nor expunged. This uniqueness, or once-for-allness, in human life gives it, in all its incompleteness, something final. It is man's fate to be born as something incomplete and to become ever more aware of this, till he dies inevitably in the same incompleteness. And nevertheless his birth, his death, and every moment of his life, have something final in them.

The relation of this to what must be said about faith is more than a mere analogy. Just because faith is concerned with man who is born once and dies once, faith is rebirth and (as we heard in Luther's words) a dying which completes this rebirth and is itself completed in physical death. However much, then, this point of view appears to agree with the view of conversion as a once-for-all event, it would be far too narrow and superficial a view of the once-for-all and definitive element in faith to restrict it to a single moment in a person's biography, instead of relating it to the whole life. This does not mean that the event of faith is to be identified with the ever new arising of the act of faith. Without a doubt this identification has grasped the important point that faith is not a quality which man possesses, nor something general apart from the here and now. It recognises that faith is something that involves responsibility and confession, and determines man concretely, something that calls for a decision, in which man's life is at stake. Even more important than all this, it recognises that faith is something that really does have finality, and is not just provisional or moving gradually to fulfilment. "If you believe, you have. If you do not believe, you do not have," says Luther (WA 7; 24). Where there is faith, there is forgiveness of sins. And "where there is forgiveness of sins, there, too, are life and blessedness," says Luther in the *Short Catechism*, on the Sacrament of the Altar. Here is salvation, God present. In principle everything is here which enables one to die in true consolation. As we said in the last lecture that time determines faith, so now we can say that faith determines time. He who believes can say at all times, "Lord, now lettest thou thy servant depart in peace, according to thy word; for mine eyes have seen thy salvation" (Luke 2.29f.). Faith is never greedy for time, as we are, who never have time, because it is never dependent upon a certain time. Nor is faith ever sick of time, as we are, who just as often wish it were past, speaking as we do, with a brutality which is no longer noticed as such, of "killing time." But for faith every time is right.

All this, then, can be said in favour of the view of faith as consisting in the constant renewal of the act of faith. And yet there is something abstract and one-sided about this.

We can clarify this objection when we remember that every

time is the time of decision, and that the question of faith or unbelief is at stake at every moment. Yet this is not apparent to men in the same way and to the same extent in each moment. In the life of every man there are exceptional situations, where he has to make a decision. They cannot be sought out as one wishes, and they can of course be missed and forgotten. The question of faith or unbelief is set for us largely, though not solely, when there is a genuine decision to be made. There are moments, not in laboured theory but in the actuality of our life, in which as it were the whole of life suddenly is focused on one point. Perhaps these moments are quite unpretentious, and their extraordinary character is perceived only by faith, in its obedience to the summons. This should lead us to a much more comprehensive view of the matter, in which we realise that however much faith is actual in the here and now, nevertheless in each concrete situation it is related to life in its entirety. Where there is faith, life, and with it birth and death, are to some extent taken up in the here and now. For faith is not concerned with this or that individual item in man, but with his being as a person—though of course with reference to this or that individual experience, deed or guilt. There is always a decision about man as such, about his ultimate and definitive being, that is, about his relation to God. Faith as an event therefore means that man as such, in the mystery of his being from his birth to his death, is in the centre of the picture. When we said that the world, or time, was the sphere of faith, it was no accident that this is the sphere of human life. In faith there is a decision about man's life. So faith may not be broken up into individual acts, but the event of faith embraces the whole of life, it takes it up into itself, and is united with it, so that for every man the history of faith becomes the history of his life, and the history of his life is the history of faith. The event of faith, which like life continues till death, is therefore to be regarded in its entirety as faith. If it is described in terms of some model of conversion, this can only be an indication of the concern of the whole life. And the event of faith, considered as life in baptism and as constant repentance, is simply the coming to faith of this human life, or better, the coming of faith to this human life. This event in which life and faith are inextricably tangled together is in reality the one event of the arising of faith. For who would ever say of himself that he has reached faith, and that its arising is now over and done with?

These considerations ought to make us aware that faith is as little capable of being systematised and exhaustively expounded as life itself. If talk about faith is to be open to the unpredictable and incalculable in life, it can have no finished model that is to be realised and imitated as the uniform type of a Christian. There must be perpetual readiness to hear the concrete demand of the word, the law and the gospel, which demands and communicates faith. Only in such terms can we speak aright of faith. Of course, what is said about faith must have its own logic. But talk about faith stays on the right lines only when all the senses are heightened to hear and understand the right word at the right time. This is when the event of faith takes place, when this hearing and watching—or, in biblical language, this watching and praying— are the way one lives in the world and in time, always alert for the concrete life of faith. And if faith is talked about—as we are doing in these reflections—this must always be something unfinished, and pointing to the sphere where the concrete life of faith is to be experienced. If you ask about faith, you must be given this kind of signpost, which in the end guides you to your own life, where alone you can really experience what faith is.

But what does experience mean in this context? We turn back to the first remarks in this lecture. If the event of faith takes place as the steadfastness of faith, then clearly experience is ranged alongside experience. But it is not the truth of faith itself which is directly experienced. For God, in whom faith trusts and on whom it builds its existence, is not himself experienced. But pure faith here trusts the promise, and holds to the Word alone. What is believed, just because it is believed, cannot be an object of experience. To this extent faith and experience are mutually exclusive. Faith believes in the face of all experience. But in confessing the truth of faith over against reality, experiences offer themselves which are peculiar to faith. Its temptations are its experiences. It is the "nevertheless" which makes faith possible. But, one might ask, are there then no victories or successes of faith, nothing that can be positively offered as an experiential proof of faith? Yes; in a certain manner, and with some reserve, it may be said that there are the experiences of freedom, peace, joy, power to love and to be patient. But who would not admit that it is precisely such experiences which can become the most severe temptation of faith, and that there is perhaps no harder test of faith than that it should overcome the temptation which arises in virtue of its victories and successes? And the most fearful temptation of all is undoubtedly to imagine that one is free of all temptation, all struggle to believe. For this would mean that one regarded oneself as exempt from faith itself. So we must hold to the fact that faith not only believes more than it experiences, but it also believes in face of all experience.

Hitherto we have spoken of temptation in the fairly indefinite sense of that which is opposed to faith. In its nature faith is always under temptation, in the sense of being opposed by something it had to resist and overcome. This can be a struggle which is full of consolation and cheerfulness, and carry the certainty of victory. But by temptation in the proper sense I mean something else, namely, that faith sees itself forsaken by what it has trusted, that the promise it clings to is experienced as a denial and a rejection. God's Yes turns into a No, the promise becomes a curse, forgiveness becomes a perpetual accusation, certainty of salvation becomes certainty of damnation, faith becomes despair. There are depths of temptation here, of which for the most part we know only by hearsay. We are readier to think of our doubts about the traditional articles of belief as temptations, or to concentrate upon our crude or our subtle moral temptations. In both spheres genuine temptations may indeed arise, even though for the most part so-called intellectual doubts do not really get to the heart of faith, and moral temptations likewise stop short of the real problem of faith.

Is it possible that our difficulty to-day in grasping what faith is, springs from the fact that we have so little real temptation? Or that we are so unfamiliar with the depths of temptation, because we are so far from faith? Is the Word of preaching so powerless, and prayer as the answer to God's Word so dumb, because we have ceased to hear the condemning voice of the law, and so cannot hear the saving Word of the gospel? Is the steadfastness of faith no longer a problem for us because we have ceased to have a living experience of faith enduring only as a miracle? Does this mean that we do not know what a miracle is because we have ceased to cry to God? Has faith a future?

XV

The Future of Faith

At the end of a discussion of the nature of faith it is natural that we should turn our eyes to the future. The last book of the Bible, the Revelation of St. John, is a grandiose fantasy of the future. The Creed adds to the preponderant majority of what sound like objects of faith in the past and the present a few with a future reference, such as Christ's coming again in judgment, the resurrection of the body, and everlasting life. Very frequently hymns, whether they are about Christmas or Passiontide, Easter or Whitsun, for morning or evening or anything else, end with an eschatological verse. And similarly works of Christian dogmatics usually end with a section on " The Last Things."

It is indeed so obvious that we should talk of the future of faith, that the question arises whether it is really necessary. Is it any more necessary than the conventional flourish at the end of some signatures, which may look well, and even ornamental, whereas in fact the name stands there without the need of any addition? Is the usual eschatological conclusion in Christian writings any different in principle from the glance at the future which you find added as a kind of appendix to many secular treatises? We know very well that such additions are not part of the serious discussion of the subject. But they go down well, for the public likes to have some indication of how the matter will continue and reach a satisfactory conclusion. Would it not be more objective and honest to forgo such anticipations of what is still to come, and under no circumstances to gloss over the fact that we know nothing about the future at all? One can of course make more or less well-established conjectures, hypothetically one can even calculate in advance, to a certain extent, if one knows the laws governing the event. The ultimate meaning of science in the service of technology is that it can make calculations and dispositions about the future—though in doing so it empties the future and dehumanises it. And where technology cannot master the future, and even perhaps produces new kinds of threat and uncertainty, we arrange insurances. And the gap that is still left, after that, in our picture of the future is filled by the assurances of the horoscope. In face of all this, should we not let the future be respected as what is simply unknown? Should we not be silent about it, instead of decorating this prospect, which is no prospect, with the gay veils of our prognoses and fantasies?

If, in spite of all these considerations, we still wish to end with the discussion of the future of faith, this must certainly not take the form of such an appendix. If that were all, then it would have been better to stop with the disturbing questions which arose at the end of the last lecture, and not to try to harmonise the dissonances by means of any theoretical last things. But we will be true to the whole style of this undertaking if we still speak of faith itself and as a whole. In each different theme I have spoken of different aspects of the one indivisible whole, and so now with the theme of "the future of faith." Far from being an appendix, this may well bring us to the heart of the matter. For faith and the future belong together. Here faith is in its element. For faith means letting the future approach. This does not ignore the fact that the future is absolutely uncertain, on the contrary it presupposes it. For faith, as absolute certainty, is in its element where it has to prove itself—namely, in what is absolutely uncertain.

Admittedly, in this theme there is a disturbing multiplicity of meanings. Three different ways lie open to us: the future of faith seen from within its own history, its eschatological future or end-history, and its present relation to the whole of the future. Each of these ways concerns faith in a different manner. The first way could be considered as analogous to the way in which we speak of "the future of the motor-car" or "the future of democracy," and so we are in the thick of prognoses about faith, whether it has a future, or whether the age of faith is past and faith is just a fossil. This is where all the anxious and confused and ignorant questions collect, questions marked by the revealing word "still": can one "still" believe in miracles, and so on— questions which assume that faith is on the way out. Even when one answers such questions with relief or with stubborn defiance, Yes, one can "still" believe this or that, the canker is in the fruit, however healthy it looks, and it is rotten within, and ready to fall.

Usually such questions about the future take the form of questions about the future of the church or of Christianity. This is perfectly justifiable. There are all kinds of alarming, and perhaps for that very reason promising, signs that what we are accustomed to call the church and Christianity are not continuing in the old, matter-of-course way that the ecclesiastical system or Christian self-consciousness seem to expect. Unfortunately, this kind of question is often asked in a party spirit, with that all too familiar modern desire for safety, and self-assertion, and at all costs remaining alive. What is the message, for what we call the church and Christianity, of these words of Jesus, " For whoever would save his life will lose it, and whoever loses his life for my sake will find it " (Matthew 16.25) ? The future of faith has a different relation to faith than the future of a party view to the party view (unless faith were already deformed to be the view of a mere Christian party). For faith is a relation to the future which concerns and determines our understanding of the future, and so changes the future itself. Faith does not merely have a future in addition to being itself. But faith is nothing else but a relation to the future. One could put it most sharply thus: faith does not "have" a future, it *is* the future.

Have we not already passed over the second way in which the future of faith may be seen? Is not this second way concerned with the future as only faith knows and confesses it? It is true that the believer does not know, any more than anyone else, what to-morrow will bring. According to the Gospel, Jesus himself who is the Son does not know the day and the hour of the end. Yet Scripture is full of utterances about the last things. We can read prophecies of what follows the end, such as the Resurrection, the judgment, and everlasting life, as well as prophecies of a series of apocalyptic signs which will precede the end. This is only partially the future for faith. For it is also the future for unbelief, the future for man, the world and history as a whole. But it would be justified to call this the "future of faith" in so far as it is a picture of the future constructed by faith.

The question at once arises whether faith has to take all this seriously, whether we can really believe the biblical prophecies. In the first place, the biblical prophecies contradict one another, and can only be swallowed whole if you do not think about them. In the second place, this starting point once again distorts faith and turns it into the appropriation of a prescribed quantity of articles of faith, which have as far as possible to be swallowed entire, no matter what effect this has on the real nature of faith. From this standpoint the eschatological sayings of the Bible would form a relatively independent part of the content of faith. Faith would have to deal with them as it also has to deal with facts of the past; and this would be the extent of its concern with the future. This would mean that at least in this respect faith would be merely a conglomeration of mythological views of the world. If there is not to be a false conflict between the nature of faith and the contents of dogmatic teaching about eschatology, the strict inner connection must be shown between the true utterance of faith and its utterances concerning the future.

Yet even if the criterion of the eschatological sayings is the nature of faith itself, this view of the future of faith is still unsatisfactory in two respects. For first, Christian faith is aware that it is directed not only towards an eschatological and final future, but also that it already shares in the accomplished eschatological event. Second, faith is aware of itself as that in which the final decision about the future is taken for everyone, so that the future is determined by faith. If we follow these indications we come anew upon the essential connection between faith and the future. And now we must add to the first two interpretations— that of the future of faith in the history of mankind, and that of the eschatological future of which faith knows—the third, that of the future of faith in the sense of the future created by faith, since it is determined and disclosed by faith. This formulation must admittedly be taken with some reserve. For if it is a matter of a connection between faith and the future, how may we talk of the future being created? Faith lives by grace, not by works; it does not achieve, but it receives and confesses the Creator; it does not wish to be Creator itself. Moreover, the future is what comes to us, for which we can only wait in patience and hope. And in the last analysis it is God who we believe is coming to us in the future: for faith his being is his coming. To glimpse the unheard-of reality that is coming to us, no timid words are sufficient. Luther dared to say of *fides* that it is *creatrix divinitatis in nobis*, faith is the creator of divinity in us (WA 40, 1; 360). So we may dare to speak of faith which creates the future.

It is surely clear that this third interpretation of our theme is the one to be followed up. Not that the two others must completely fall out. But what is fundamental for a responsible and clear understanding is the nature of this relation between the future and faith, in other words, how it is that the future arises out of faith.

That it is the nature of faith to be related to the future is already established when we realise that faith justifies, and is therefore faith to salvation. Faith grasps the promise that God is for us, and therefore it knows that nothing can be against us. The justified man has peace with God, and he who is sheltered in God's peace need have no care about the future. The believer shares in the omnipotence of God, and whatever else this may mean, in the first instance it means that nothing can tear him from God's hands, but he has been decided about for all eternity. He has his home and dwelling place, though in this life he still has his place in the world, in a foreign land. Whatever the various ways in which this may be described or expressed, faith is essentially this certainty concerning the future of one's life, this confident trust that cannot be disappointed or confuted by any future event. Faith is not a pre-condition of salvation, but is the certainty of it; and as such it is itself the event of salvation. Faith which cannot be called salvation-faith in this way is not faith. Hence the word which awakens faith and to which faith clings, for it lives by it, is the word which opens up the future, it is the word of promise, not the word of the law which clings to the past. And whatever the direction in which faith expresses itself and makes its confession, it always includes this confession of the future which has been opened to it. If it confesses God as Creator, then however much it may think of an event of the past, the creation of the world, it essentially means the futurity which is included in this event, which is the future of faith. It means the word of promise which communicates this event, which is the word of faith. Or if faith looks to the crucified Jesus, it has indeed a historical fact of the past in view. But faith is present only so far as the future arises out of this, and the promise, and the saving and final word, which nothing can hold back, and which is valid once for all. An irrefutable criterion for all talk about faith is the question, What has it to do with the future? To what extent is the future promised in it? To what extent does the future take place in it?

But we must examine more precisely what the future means. Here we must pay heed to a rule which holds good of all talk about faith. We can only speak of faith with the aid of words that we use generally in life, quite apart from faith. This is not, as is often supposed, a regrettable necessity, making the language of faith unreal, obscure and symbolic. This is a quite wrong view. What faith has to say it says in the most real and direct manner. What it has to speak of it communicates with a precision that leaves nothing to be desired. The language of faith is not the most indirect, but on the contrary the most direct use that can be made of language. And this is so, because faith, as we have repeatedly said, speaks of our real life. It is not suspended in a dream world, but its sphere is the world and time. So the language of faith is the language in which this world and this time are expressed. Faith would cease to be faith if it used a special language of its own, and not the language of the world and of time. But faith clearly speaks of the world and time in a different way from the usual. And the words faith lays claim to acquire a different meaning from their normal usage. If in the context of faith I speak of God, this word "God" has a quite different meaning from what it would have outside this context. Similarly, if I speak from the standpoint of faith about the world, the meaning of the word "world" also changes. And if I speak of the future in relation to faith, this word "future" acquires a new meaning.

Here, then, is the decisive rule in the grammar of faith. This change in the sense of words must on no account lead to the construction of a special and esoteric language of faith. As I have already indicated, this would spell the death of faith. Not only would faith then be incommunicable to the uninitiated. For how could they understand this special esoteric language? But further, faith itself would thereby be separated and cut off from the world and time. It would have removed itself from temptation. But as we have seen, faith which escapes from temptation ceases to be faith. Faith does not die of temptation, but of the flight from temptation.

But what has this to do with the language of faith? The new meanings which words gain from faith do not lose touch with their old meanings, which they have apart from faith. And this produces a twofold situation, such as you find in all genuine discussion (rare though it is): at one and the same time you understand the language of the other and you contradict it. In the language of faith you see the effect of faith being always under temptation. For a proper understanding and interpretation of the language of faith the conflict which is concealed within it must be brought to light, and it must be made clear just where the victory of faith over unbelief is expected. A genuine utterance of faith must always be capable of a fighting interpretation. A word that cannot be used as a sword against unbelief is not the Word of God. " For the word of God is living and active, sharper than any two-edged sword, piercing to the division of soul and spirit, of joints and marrow, and discerning the thoughts and intentions of the heart. And before him no creature is hidden, but all are open and laid bare to the eyes of him with whom we have to do " (Hebrews 4.12f.). Every word must be interpreted in such a fashion that it also expresses unbelief. The speech of faith must outstrip the speech of unbelief, that is, it must set the event of speech in motion.

What, then, is the meaning of "the future"? It would be super-ficial to define it merely as the continuation in time beyond the present. We do not need to appeal to faith in order to show the inadequacy of this interpretation. The future is not an empty space stretching out ahead of me, entry into which is more or less settled of itself, as a stone enters to-morrow from to-day without its doing anything or having anything done to it. But it is of the nature of the future that man knows that he is approached by it, and himself approaches it, in hope or care or some other relation. The depths of the future can be glimpsed only in relation to human existence.

Characteristically, in respect of the future we speak of awaiting in the twofold sense, that this and that awaits us, and that we await or expect this and that. In this traffic of awaiting and being awaited there is realised the traffic of speech, of our conversation, passionate or bored, wrathful or patient, cursing or blessing, with what awaits and approaches us. If we think what it is that occasions speech in man, what kind of being spoken to impels him to speak, then his conversation with the future must be given a decisive place. The word "conversation" may awaken false notions. For we mean a call and crying, as well as a quiet whisper, we mean laughing and weeping, accusation and self-defence, sometimes a terrified speechlessness, and also complete silence. The radical interpretation of this confusion of voices, and failure of all speech, in the relation between man and the future is to be found at the point which is like a mathematical point, where everything meets, namely, the conscience. The future is not an empty stretch of time, but that which is still to come and is already stirring in the conscience.

We are approaching the point where ultimate decisions have to be taken in the struggle to understand the future. We can put it quite simply: is there nothing left, is man finished and balanced and purified, when there is no more time left? Has death the last word, in the sense that the man who is falling silent in death is asked nothing more, and has nothing more to say? Or is there a word which disputes the last word with death, and which matters for the dying or the dead man, and calls to him as the man he was, even if his last hour has struck? Or we could put it thus:

what is the real future of the future? Is it death, or is it God?

Faith confesses that God is the future, and so it does not shun death. It does not shun temptation. If you believe, you do not run away. This does not just become acute at the end. But throughout one's life the relation to the future is determined by this. It is as though faith wakened you from sleep. If you confess God as the future, then the future becomes quite different, even though and just because you have the same future before you as everyone else of your time. Faith creates a new and true future, in that while enduring this human, all too human, future, it praises God as *the* future, and so transforms the face of this human future. We could also formulate this, in relation to what we have said about the conscience, in the following words: faith makes the future a blessing and not a curse. For the conscience that is confident in faith is able to bless the temporal. And to be able to do this, to bless all that is in time, demands much, incredibly much. For this we need to look at him who accomplished it as man. The meaning of the future has been revealed and expressed once for all by the Crucified One.

Is it matter for regret that we have provided no detailed discussion either of the many special problems of eschatology or of the question of the historical future of Christian faith? These are certainly not the only subjects which we have failed to treat fully and adequately. But at least we may hope that the attentive reader will not now have to sail without a compass across a sea of problems. Even if the questions have now become much more difficult for many than they first realised, yet perhaps a beginning can be seen from which everything can become quite simple again. If that is the case, then they have begun to hear in a new way. And this would bring us to the point where the whole discussion is intended to lead us, to the source of faith. For faith comes from hearing, that is, from the communication of faith (Romans 10.17).

The Word of God and Language

This subject raises many questions. We must stop short at the first words, and ask what "the Word of God" means. Is this more than a form of words? Can the Word of God really encounter us? "Language" is another matter. This does not seem to be a remote, obscure or dubious entity. But everyone has it, for man is the being who has language. Of course language can fail him: knowledge of language does not protect him from sudden speechlessness. Nor is the language of authority learned in a language course. So here, too, there are problems which lead far, even if one is ignorant of the present state of the discussion of the problem of language, in which all the questions about the world and man and history are increasingly concentrated. Is it possible that the two great complexes of questions contained in our theme stand in such a relation to one another that the question of the "Word of God" may help to elucidate the problems of language?

But the immediate problem is the reverse of this: not whether the Word of God can throw light on the vexatious problems of language, but the fact that the Word of God itself has clearly become a vexatious problem of language. It is at this point that the opposed views come into touch with one another, of those who expect nothing from the Word of God, and of those who expect the decisive thing.

The first group takes it as settled that the Word of God cannot enter language, and therefore that it means nothing. For what cannot enter language is not there, at any rate for us; it is no more than an alleged word, which cannot enter language. " The Word of God," it is said, is a mythical expression, which is over and done with. For how is one to imagine God as speaking? And if speaking, in what language? Has God a language of his own? If so, we could neither understand it nor say anything about it. But supposing we could learn something of it by means of some mysterious device of translation, would it be any more than an indirect and symbolic reflection, not the literal Word of God, but merely human words with the doubtful claim to be the Word of God? In earlier times men may have been able to take this concept seriously, and not to doubt that the Word of God could enter language. But to-day, so runs the argument, this cannot honestly be done. The nature of language prevents it. There is a wide range of views, both superficial and profound, both carefully thought out and merely emotional, both impious and pious, which are united in their agreement that the Word of God and language are mutually exclusive.

But there is another group who cannot rid themselves of this question of the Word of God. They are not to be confused with those who use the phrase thoughtlessly. For they know of the difficulty, the disturbance in the relation between the Word of God and language. But their starting-point is the certainty that the Word of God has entered language, and they live in the certain expectation that it desires to do so and will do so. They do not push the question aside, what the Word of God means, but their first concern is what has been handed down as the Word of God. By this they mean the Bible. And this is not just a book and no more, but the central point, from history to history, from experience to experience, from faith to faith. The Bible bears witness to a proclamation which has taken place and is the impulse to a proclamation which is to take place. And this event, which claims to be the Word of God, is not mere speech. But it sets something in motion, just as it itself was set in motion. It has to do with reality, which it changes.

This, then, is what is seen by those who cannot rid themselves of the question of the Word of God. It is knowledge, with something of their own experience attached to it. But they are also aware that this event of proclamation is not an event any more to-day, but largely just talk, in which the claim of the Word of God is no longer heard; it is proclamation in a form of language which has become incomprehensible, it is a mere recitation of the traditional Word of God, in which the Word of God does not enter language in the present.

What is so deeply disturbing to many Christians to-day, when they consider the commission of the church and the nature of their faith, and what is so painfully confirmed by what they hear of preaching and teaching, has probably been better put by Dietrich Bonhoeffer than by anyone else. In 1944, less than a year before his execution, he wrote from prison: " We have been thrown back once more to the beginnings of understanding. The meaning of reconciliation and salvation, of rebirth and the Holy Spirit, of loving your enemy, of the cross and the resurrection, of life in Christ and discipleship, are all so remote and strange that we scarcely dare to speak of them any more. In the traditional words and actions we glimpse something new and revolutionary, without being able to grasp it and express it. This is our own fault."

For a church whose goal is in itself is, according to Bonhoeffer, "incapable of being the bearer of the reconciling and saving word for men and for the world. That is why the old words fail and fall silent, and our Christian life consists only of prayer and doing the right thing among men." But this is just where there is hope that the Word of God may enter language once more. Bonhoeffer writes, "It is not for us to foretell the day, but the day will come when men will be called to utter the Word of God in such a way that the world is changed and renewed. There will be a new language, perhaps quite unreligious, but liberating and saving, like the language of Jesus, so that men are horrified at it, and yet conquered by its power: the language of a new righteousness and truth, the language which tells of the peace of God and the coming of his kingdom " (cf. *Letters and Papers from Prison* Fontana edition, p. 160).

The effects of these two views are opposed. They are divided on the question of the future of the Word of God in relation to language. But they are also in close touch with one another. They are both profoundly dissatisfied with present-day proclamation of the Word of God. Both groups say that the language spoken there does not correspond to the claim which is made. Both acknowledge that they find largely incomprehensible what is presented there with all the appearance of being a matter of course. That in spite of this the two groups reach such a very different judgment perhaps indicates that a conversation between them would be not amiss. The judgment of the first group, that the Word of God cannot really enter language, clearly rests upon quite different presuppositions and conceptions than the expectation of the second group that the Word of God, which has entered language, will do so anew. The first group rejects as mythological that which the second group by no means regards as such. And on the other hand, Bonhoeffer's words about a new language, "perhaps quite unreligious, but liberating and saving," undoubtedly strikes a chord with those who thought that the question of the Word of God and language was over and done with.

It may be helpful to consider some points of view concerning the relation of word and language in general. By "word" we do not mean the single word. This word, as a unit of language, is an abstraction over against the original conception of word as containing an encounter. By "word," then, we mean something with a totality of meaning. Further, it is likewise an abstraction to limit "word" to its significant content. In the multitude of written and printed words we must not forget that it is the speaking of words which discloses their real nature, something that happens, by word of mouth. The basic model for this event is not a statement, irrespective of the situation of speaking. It would be better to describe the event of the word as a communication. For words take place between two partners, they make participation possible, they create communication. Certainly it matters what the content and significance of the communication is. Yet the same words can in different situations with different persons entirely change their meaning. Thus our usual understanding of communication is too narrow to grasp the event in its entirety. The power of words as communication is by no means restricted to information and the increase of knowledge. The power of words as an event is that they can touch and change our very life, when one man tells another, and thus shares with another, something of his own life, his willing and loving and hoping, his joy and sorrow, but also his hardness and hates, his meanness and wickedness.

The extremes of the concrete word (what he calls the "tongue") have been powerfully depicted in the Epistle of James: "With it we bless the Lord and Father, and with it we curse men, who are made in the likeness of God. From the same mouth come blessing and cursing" (James 3.9-10). But there is no thought of a balance here. The emphasis lies on horror at the demonic power of the word. "So the tongue is a little member and boasts of great things. How great a forest is set ablaze by a small fire! And the tongue is a fire. The tongue is an unrighteous world among our members, staining the whole body, setting on fire the cycle of nature, and set on fire by hell. For every kind of beast and bird, of reptile and sea creature, can be tamed and has been tamed by humankind, but no human being can tame the tongue—a restless evil, full of deadly poison" (James 3.5-8).

The word clearly means man himself, who is able to be lord of the whole world, only not of himself. So Jesus asks, "How can you speak good, when you are evil? For out of the abundance of the heart the mouth speaks" (Matthew 12.34). So he emphasises with surprising sharpness our responsibility for what we say: "I tell you, on the day of judgment men will render account for every careless word they utter; for by your words you will be justified, and by your words you will be condemned" (Matthew 12.36f.).

So we do not get at the nature of words by asking what they contain, but by asking what they effect, what they set going, what future they disclose. How much words belong to man and, like human life, are historical, may be seen in the fact that the discussion of words becomes a discussion of their future, and thus of man's future. The highest thing that words could achieve would be to disclose the true future. But where are such words to be found?

Let us now consider language and its relations to words. It is no accident that we at once think of the multiplicity of languages, of our native language and of foreign languages. A universal language can only be a bloodless and technical contrivance. Languages are highly complicated traditional structures which have grown over centuries and millennia, in which the many layers of historical life have been deposited and which—so far as living languages are concerned—continue their slow and steady change. He who wishes to speak must choose a language, or normally has a language chosen for him by birth and upbringing.

In that a language is spoken the problem of understanding at once arises. For language, which makes understanding possible for one man, prevents understanding for another. Language creates simultaneously understanding and incomprehension, it binds and it separates. Admittedly, language is not exactly like a completely sealed vessel. What goes on in a language is a human phenomenon which crosses the boundaries of language, and so can be translated. But this cannot be done in the way one pours water from one vessel to another. Translation is an art; but even when it is done in a masterly fashion, it is still a change. For what is spoken has been thought in terms of a specific language. To put it into another language means to think it through afresh.

Languages are differentiated from one another by their spirit. Different ways of meeting reality and of understanding it have found expression in them. For the history of Christianity, as well as of the West (which are by no means identical), the difference between Greek and Hebrew has been of immense significance in view of their encounter with one another. Language is much more than a system of words and grammatical rules. Moreover, differentiation of language extends much further than division into different national languages. There are connections which cut across such divisions. The language of science is not the language of love. And the language, say, of Aristotle preserves its characteristic nature through every translation; similarly with the language of the Bible or with certain parts of it, such as the language of Jesus. Our dependence on linguistic tradition means far more than that we have to make use of some formal means of communication. But actually we live on the reality that is disclosed to us by language, and on the immense wealth that is handed down to us, and on which our speech draws. Language opens up the space to us in which the event of the word can take place. So we carry responsibility for language in what we say. And when the event of the word is an extraordinary one, it is creative of language, that is, it creates new possibilities of addressing and understanding the reality which approaches us, and becomes the source of light which can again and again lighten up the darkness of existence.

This is the direction indicated for us in God's Word, " Thy

word is a lamp to my feet and a light to my path" (Psalm 119.105). There is no problem here about how God's Word can be encountered in human words. For God's Word here means simply the Word—the pure and true Word, in which the real life and purpose of the Word is realised. This means the Word as man needs it—the good Word which he needs more than food and drink. So it is the Word which it concerns every man to utter and to answer. For this is the true and wholesome and real use of the Word. The Word is meant to illuminate, to disclose understanding, not only in its outward function, but most important of all in relation to the way which is to be gone. The Word is meant to open the future. Why then is it called God's Word, when it is no strange and superhuman act, but such a truly human word?

Now it is undoubtedly appropriate to speak of the Word of God in the sharpest opposition to the words that are spoken among men. For this good, beneficent, saving, illuminating Word, which discloses the true future, is not normally to be encountered. Men owe it to one another, they fail to say it, and they experience in themselves how it is not said to them. And where that Word really does happen, men fail it, because it disappoints their expectations and contradicts their desires. For it is the pure Word in this sense, that it expects faith, that faith which relies on the promise alone.

On what promise? The promise of God. A promise means a pledge from one to another regarding the future. The Word as an event is always something said from one to another, as it were he carries his saying to the other, so that it is with him, or he is with the matter which is being spoken about. The Word which is concerned with God would then in this sense say God to us, so that God comes to the one addressed and is with him, and the one addressed is with God. All talk of God in which this does not happen would not be real talk of God.

The Word receives the most explicit character of a promise when the future of the one addressed is involved, and the speaker himself does not promise this or that, but himself, pledges himself and his own future for the future of the other, gives him his word in the full sense of giving a share in himself. And here is the reason for the ultimate failure of the Word among men. For what happens when one man promises himself to the other? For the most part the Word becomes the bearer and mediator of egotism, inner emptiness, or lies. Yet even at his best man cannot promise true future, that is, salvation, to the other. Only the Word by which God comes to man, and promises himself, is able to do this. That this Word has happened, and can therefore be spoken again and again, that a man can therefore promise God to another as the One who promises himself—this is the certainty of Christian faith. And this is the true and fulfilled event of the Word, when space is made among men for this promise, this Word of God.

When God speaks, the whole of reality as it concerns us enters language anew. God's Word does not bring God into language in isolation. It is not a light which shines upon God, but a light which shines from him, illumining the sphere of our existence. If God's countenance shines upon us, the world has for us another look. The world, as the reality which concerns us, in whatever language it has hitherto been expressed, is the call and question of God to us, even though we do not understand. Hence human words are, at their most profound, always answers. Man speaks because he is addressed. Language is the manifold echo to the question of God. So the event of the Word of God is necessarily bound up with the entire life of language. For if the Word of God brings the whole of our reality into language anew, then the reality which is already in language is necessarily addressed anew.

This touches the root of the vexatious linguistic problem in the Word of God. The happening of the Word of God has created a linguistic tradition of its own, to be seen not only in many forms in the Bible, but also in great variety and indeed disharmony in the history of the church. And now the Word of God, with this tradition, wishes to aim at reality in present-day language, it wants to express it anew and so express itself anew. The difficulty is only apparently solved by the manipulation of language, by modernising words and making use of fashionable jargon. God's Word is expressed anew only when it is heard anew, with tense attention to how the traditional Word manages to make itself understood in the real circumstances to which our lives are exposed. This listening combines two things in one: an upright perseverance in experience, and a patient waiting upon understanding. If the Word of God were heard anew in this way, it could also be spoken anew with the authority proper to it. And that would transform our linguistic problem; for though this seems to be a linguistic problem for the Word of God, it is in truth our own linguistic dilemma.